THE SCOTTISH NATION

THE SCOTTISH NATION

Edited by Gordon Menzies

BRITISH BROADCASTING CORPORATION

020113

941
MEN

First published 1972
Published by the British Broadcasting Corporation
35, Marylebone High Street, London W1M 4AA
Printed in England by Tonbridge Printers Ltd., Tonbridge, Kent
ISBN : 0 563 10685 9

Eworth: Detail from *Henry Stewart, Lord Darnley and his Brother Charles Stewart, Earl of Lennox* (plate 21). Reproduced by gracious permission of Her Majesty the Queen.

Acknowledgment is due to the following for permission to reproduce photographs:

ASHMOLEAN MUSEUM, OXFORD Battle of Dunbar (plate 33); BIBLIOTHEQUE MUNICIPALE D'ARRAS (photo Giraudon) Sir Bernard Stewart (plate 7); BRITISH MUSEUM Battle of Flodden (plate 14); DEPARTMENT OF THE ENVIRONMENT (crown copyright) Caerlaverock Castle (plate 1), Lochindorb Castle (plate 3), Elgin Cathedral (plate 4), Tomb of the Wolf of Badenoch (plate 5), Angel figures, Rosslyn Chapel (plate 9), Holyrood Palace (plate 12), Chapel Royal, Falkland Palace (plate 16), Lochleven Castle (plate 22), Hermitage Castle (plate 24), Linlithgow Palace (plate 27), Crichton Castle (plate 28), Earl Patrick's Palace (plate 29); EDINBURGH PUBLIC LIBRARIES Slezer's Prospect of Perth (plate 38); MARQUIS OF BUTE Bute Mazer (plate 2); NATIONAL MUSEUM OF ANTIQUITIES OF SCOTLAND James III coin (plate 8), Fetternear Banner (plate 18), late 17th Century silverware (plate 37), The Riding of Parliament (plate 39); NATIONAL PORTRAIT GALLERY George Buchanan (plate 26); ROYAL COMMISSION ON THE ANCIENT AND HISTORICAL MONUMENTS OF SCOTLAND Stirling heads (cover), Kinross House (plate 34), Crathes Castle (plate 36); ROYAL SCOTTISH MUSEUM The Great Michael (plate 13); SCOTTISH FIELD AND MR P. MAXWELL-STUART Rosary and Crucifix (plate 20); SCOTTISH NATIONAL LIBRARY Andrew Myllar's printing device (plate 11); SCOTTISH NATIONAL PORTRAIT GALLERY James V and Mary of Guise (plate 15), 2nd Earl of Arran (plate 17), Mary Queen of Scots (plate 19), John Knox (plate 23), James VI (plate 25), 1st Marquis of Montrose (plate 30), 1st Marquis of Argyll (plate 31), Execution of Charles I (plate 32), 1st Duke of Lauderdale (plate 35); COLONEL STIRLING OF KEIR James IV (plate 10); J. K. ST. JOSEPH, CAMBRIDGE UNIVERSITY COLLECTION Threave Castle (plate 6).

The maps were drawn by Brian and Constance Dear.

Contents

Illustrations

Fig 1 Genealogical Tree

Fig 2 Scotland in 1707

Foreword

The Scottish Nation was conceived as a television series, produced by BBC Scotland, as a sequel to *Who are the Scots?* And, as in the case of *Who are the Scots?*, it was felt that some more permanent record should be provided to accompany the television presentation of this unique period in Scotland's history. From 1296 to 1707 it can be claimed with some constitutional accuracy that Scotland, was, indeed, a nation.

Scottish history is much more than the dreary 'long brawl' that is often suggested. Of course, there were brawling nobles and weak kings. No doubt there were many examples of political ineptitude, internecine strife and brutality in the name of religion. But what country in Europe was free of similar problems in medieval and early modern times? Certainly not England where in the turbulent fourteenth and fifteenth centuries no less than five kings – Edward II, Richard II, Henry VI, Edward V and Richard III – were either murdered or assassinated, compared to only two in Scotland – James I and James III. On the other hand, Scotland was cursed by a succession of royal minorities. Perhaps it was politically weak and economically backward but it was always different and seldom impotent.

The relationship with England is the key factor in the birth, growth and, perhaps, the decline of the Scottish nation. From Edward I through the centuries and on to the unions of crown and parliament Anglo/Scottish relations are ever significant in the life of the Scottish nation. To the English, Scotland was a recalcitrant northern neighbour, a perennial thistle in their flesh. English efforts to bring the Scots into their political orbit did more to fan the flame of Scottish patriotism than anything else.

Yet Scotland is more than one nation. Highlands have always been different from Lowlands. Any aspirations that the Celtic peoples of the north and west had of extending their sway to the rest of Scotland were dimmed by the intrusions of the Anglo/Norman feudal nobility in the twelfth and thirteenth centuries. It took another four centuries and some thousands of lives before they were finally brought under royal control. But Gaelic culture survived and continued to flourish alongside that of the alien Scots of the Lowland areas. Meanwhile the newer Scottish culture, akin to English in some respects yet so different in others, was also developing until it flowered in the late fifteenth and early sixteenth centuries. In any roll of honour for the Scottish nation Henryson, Dunbar and Gavin Douglas deserve a place alongside Wallace, Bruce, James VI and Montrose.

Many people within the BBC itself have contributed to the preparation of this book and I am grateful for their advice, guidance and attention to detail. I have constantly been encouraged by the infectious enthusiasm and inquiring mind of Dr Ian Grimble, the presenter of the related television series. I am especially grateful to Professor Gordon Donaldson, who helped me to break down this period of Scotland's past into ten programmes and ten chapters. We did not attempt to produce a comprehensive coverage but to select what we considered to be the main themes and the principal personalities, with the overall aim of encouraging more people to take an intelligent interest in the heritage of one of Europe's oldest nations. I have conceived my task as editor of this book as one of streamlining the various contributions, of standardising spelling and terminology, and of avoiding obvious overlaps between the chapters. The views expressed are those of the individual contributors and I have made no attempt to edit out opinion or to damp down controversy.

If the Scottish nation did come to an end in 1707 it bequeathed to posterity a social, cultural and religious heritage that is still part of our national life. The most perplexing quest for man is the search for his own identity. The Scot will find part of the answer in the history of his nation, in the struggles, the anguish and the achievements of Scots men and women which did so much to mould the Scottish character. The Scottish nation may have passed into history but 'Scotland' and 'Scots' are still terms which have their own distinctive national meaning.

GORDON MENZIES

CHAPTER I

Wars of Independence

G. W. S. Barrow

On a night of storm in March 1286 Scotland lost the last king of her ancient dynasty, Alexander III. Ten years later, almost to the day, his kingdom was plunged into war with England, her larger and richer neighbour to the south, a war which was to endure with comparatively brief intervals of peace or truce till the fifteenth century. These long years of war and hardship gave the Scottish nation a consciousness of its own identity stronger than anything previously known. Yet the name usually given to them, the 'Wars of Independence', is a misleading modernism, which would have seemed incomprehensible to Scots of the thirteenth or fourteenth centuries. Far from coming to a sudden awareness of their separate identity in 1296 and striving to throw off long centuries of foreign rule, the Scots were alarmed at the prospect of their ancient and separate kingdom being relegated to the status of a feudal barony held by the English Crown or, worse still, being perhaps abolished or at least swallowed up by a more powerful and recognisably different political lordship. It would be truer to call them the 'wars of preservation', or even 'wars of conservation'.

Undeniably, a sense of nationalism was accelerated in both Scotland and England at the turn of the thirteenth and fourteenth centuries by the wars waged between the English Edwards and the Scots kings, Balliol and Bruce. But nationalism was already an irreversible tide in European history. It was an accident, indeed quite literally an accident, which made the Anglo-Scottish wars one of the earliest test-beds of conflicting nationalism. Nevertheless, with hindsight we can justifiably say that despite long years of peace and friendly relations the kingdoms of England and Scotland were shaping inexorably, during the thirteenth century, towards a conflict which would be different from the old, almost casual, feudal strife, which would in fact be more profound, more bitter, and much more difficult to resolve. European kingship of the high middle ages had, it is true, emerged out of feudalism; but it had taken on a vigorous life of its own, drawing its strength from a balance between external aggression and internal peace-keeping and law-giving. Slowly, but very surely, the west European monarchies became 'national'. The more 'national' they were the more successful they were and, barring accidents, the longer they were likely to survive.

Barring accidents; there was the rub. The Capetian dynasty of France, a perfect example of a monarchy which had first adapted itself to feudalism and then adapted itself to nationalism, was at the height of its power and prestige when in 1328 Charles IV died and, for the first time for over three hundred years, there was no direct male heir of the Capets. More than a century passed before the French monarchy became effectively 'national' once more. Succession problems have always been the classic starting-point of far-reaching conflicts which have had little or nothing to do with the technical details of succession itself. So it proved with Scotland in 1286. King Alexander's heir, acknowledged by the Scots lords in a remarkable proof of their political maturity, was King Eric of Norway's little daughter Margaret. By 1290 plans for her to marry the heir to the English throne, Edward of Caernarvon, were complete. A cautiously defensive marriage treaty had been ratified (Birgham-Northampton) and it is clear from its contents that it had been drafted largely by the Scots with the purpose of protecting the separate identity and special interests of the Scottish kingdom. All these plans, with their mixture of hopefulness and mistrust, were frustrated when the Maid of Norway died on her way to Scotland. King Edward I, called upon to preside over a settlement of claims to the Scots throne put in by thirteen competitors, insisted upon his 'superior lordship' over the northern kingdom being acknowledged by all the parties, and particularly, once the choice had fallen (no doubt correctly) on John Balliol, by the new king of Scots himself (December 1292).

Even if Edward I's demands had been of the most perfunctory and nominal kind, King John's position would have been difficult. But the English king insisted on the spirit and the letter of feudal law and something more besides. This misjudgement is all the more remarkable in a man who in these same years could rouse the patriotism of his own people with the warning that the king of France was bent upon the invasion of England and had threatened to 'wipe out the English nation from its land, if his power were equal to a scheme of such horrible iniquity, which God forbid'. The Scots magnates – bishops, earls and great barons – had already come to see themselves as the natural leaders of a 'community of the realm' of Scotland. The phrase, while it could bear different shades of meaning, is best understood as denoting the corporate unity of the kingdom and its people insofar as this was not, or for some reason could not be, comprehended in the king himself. As the wretched Balliol was pricked harder and harder by the feudal goad, the Scots plough which he had been elected to pull took on a life of its own, dug itself in, and refused to cut the furrow mapped out for it by the masterful King Edward. A council of twelve took the government of Scotland out of King John's hands, appealing to the papacy for moral, to the king of France for physical, support (July 1295–February 1296).

King Edward's fury evidently reflected the extent to which he had misjudged the Scottish situation. A large English army crossed into Scotland at Coldstream on 28 March 1296 and moved down the Tweed to take and sack Berwick, Scotland's richest town, with much slaughter and destruction. A month later King John's own army, the chivalry of Scotland reinforced by a sizeable infantry force, was scattered with heavy loss on a hillside south of Dunbar. The English advanced methodically northward, securing castle after castle and driving the hapless Scottish king and his now discredited councillors before them until they were forced to surrender early in July, at Brechin and Montrose. King Edward pressed on as far as Elgin, displaying the English royal banner farther north than it had ever been seen before. While King John, who had been compelled to abdicate, was led ignominiously to captivity in the Tower of London, the English forces scoured wide areas of the central and eastern highlands before returning south for a great 'reconstruction' parliament at Berwick in August. At this parliament an English administration for Scotland was established, and almost two thousand of the more substantial and prominent Scotsmen and Scotswomen gave in their fealty and homage to the English king – though it is unlikely that more than a small proportion of this great roll-call actually came to Berwick to perform the ceremonies in person. Even so, that summer had witnessed an impressive demonstration of King Edward's power and an apparent vindication of his belief that the kingdom of Scotland – which he had not yet abolished – was properly subordinate to the crown of England and would remain so.

With the next two years a pattern emerged which was to repeat itself again and again in Anglo-Scottish relations. Against a fairly consistent background of English demands for suzerainty over Scotland a number of elements or groups may be distinguished in the Scottish foreground. On the one hand, there were a few great nobles and gentry, presumably with their dependants, who saw English overlordship as a permanent reality – for whom, in other words, Edward I and the Plantagenets had effectively taken the place of the vanished Scottish dynasty of former ages. Two earls of Dunbar (until 1315) belonged to this group, and so, invariably, did the earls of Angus, who were de Umfravilles from Northumberland. Comparable with this small group, yet in a significantly different position, were a number of the nobles from the Isle of Man, the Hebrides and the west Highland seaboard, who had not yet become reconciled to the fact that since 1266 this wide region had been brought within the Scottish kingdom and must look to Perth and Edinburgh for its government rather than Bergen or (more often than not) to nowhere in particular. Such were the Macdougalls, lords of Lorn, the senior representative of the great house of Somerled (d. 1164), certain individuals among their kinsmen the Macruaries and Macdonalds, and a few powerful families of the west who had close links with Ireland, such as the Macsweens of Knapdale, builders of Castle Sween. These west highlanders and islanders can hardly be seen as especially 'pro-English', at least not on principle; rather were they suspicious of and hostile to effective royal government in the west from whatever source it might come. And in any case, their attitude was greatly complicated by the fierce rivalry among the descendants of Somerled which was a dominant feature of Hebridean politics until the 'lordship of the Isles' became a reality in the later fourteenth century.

The majority of Scots nobles, despite their homage to Edward I in 1291 and 1296 which they were very soon to explain away as having been taken under duress, seem to have believed that the kingdom of Scotland, as they and their forebears had experienced it in the twelfth and thirteenth centuries, not only had a right to exist but would survive military defeat and the fall of King John. They were, however, divided in at least two ways. First, there were the handful of the greatest nobility, the dozen or so earls and one or two others such as the hereditary steward – the 'Stewart' – and the lords of Annandale (Bruce), Badenoch (Comyn) and Douglas

(Douglas). These great magnates were unaboidably close to the crown, whether Scottish or English, and many of them had English possessions. They were ill-equipped for any but the most formal, feudal kind of war and if they were defeated their education had trained them to accept defeat. Below them, and often attached to them by tenure, affinity or that personal service which made many young men join a great lord's 'meiny' or following were the lesser lairds, gentry and substantial freeholders. In Scotland a much higher proportion of this class were tenants-in-chief of the crown than in England. One of the most striking facts about Scotland after 1296 is that most of these men did not immediately switch their traditional allegiance to the crown to Edward I and his son. On the contrary, they quickly became the very mainstay of the Scottish struggle against English rule. Sir Thomas Maule of Panmure held Brechin Castle against Edward I in 1303 when much Scottish resistance had elsewhere collapsed. Sir William Oliphant, whose defence of Stirling Castle in 1304 forms one of the most splendid chapters of British military history, insisted that he held his command 'of the Lyon', that is, of the Crown of Scotland. A Berwickshire knight, William de Vieuxpont, was arrested at Blaye near Bordeaux in 1300 while spying on English shipping movements; he was said to be 'of the company of William Wallace'. In 1306 Sir Malcolm of Innerpeffray, a vassal of the earl of Strathearn, was as conspicuously bold and prompt to support Robert Bruce's bid for the throne as his lord was tardy and timid. A few years later, three lairds from very different parts of Scotland, Gilbert Hay of Errol, Neil Campbell of Lochawe and Alexander Seton of Seton, met near Stirling and swore a solemn oath to defend the liberty of the Scottish kingdom, and of its recently crowned king Robert I, against all mortal men, French, English or Scots, 'until the last moment of their lives'. Towering above the rest, of course, yet coming from the selfsame *milieu* in Scottish society, is the great figure of William Wallace, who stood out in 1297 as the champion of the community of the realm and of what he also called 'the liberty of the kingdom'. Wallace was a son of the tenant of Elderslie, beside Paisley, a small fief held of the Stewart as part of his great lordship of Renfrew. The Stewart and the bishop of Glasgow were in fact Wallace's earliest patrons, but he soon showed that he would take a very independent and much bolder course of action.

As well as this horizontal division among the Scots nobles there was a more damaging vertical division. Despite the church's exhortations and the law's sanctions, feuds and vendettas (certainly not peculiar to Scotland) were endemic. But among the Scots they were especially bitter and intractable after 1292 since they were inextricably bound up with the dispute over the succession. Balliol *versus* Bruce was also, often automatically, Comyn *versus* Stewart, Macdougall *versus* Macdonald, Abernethy, Buchan, Ross, Strathearn *versus* Atholl, Douglas, Mar and Soulis. From 1296 to 1308 the war of the Scots against the English was at the same time an internal struggle, sometimes actually a fierce civil war, to settle the question of whether the great family of Comyn, dominant for much of the thirteenth century, should keep its old lead in Scots affairs, or whether the smaller family of Bruce with its many powerful allies should oust the Comyns once and for all. In the end, as every schoolboy knows, the Bruces emerged triumphant; but not without the struggle leaving behind it a legacy of internecine bitterness which it would take many generations and many more years of English hostility to efface.

The two last groups to be considered in the Scottish pattern are the church and non-noble class, burgesses, small farmers, servants of various kinds, pastoralists and fishermen, the landless and the unfree. Contrary to a belief about the medieval church which is still widely held, the Scots clergy of this period did not speak with a single voice, nor did they rise above the feuds and squabbles which beset the laity. Indeed, the church no longer enjoyed the almost unchallenged moral authority which it had possessed in the twelfth century. At the same time, it remained an indispensable and enormously influential part of society. Its leaders, the bishops and the greater abbots, took a natural place in the counsels of the community of the realm, and its highly trained administrators, lawyers and writers were expected to put their skill at the service of government. The six regents or 'Guardians' who had governed Scotland from 1286 to 1291 included two bishops, and not only these Guardians but their successors, Balliol's council of twelve, William Wallace in 1297, and the various combinations of nobles and ecclesiastics who followed Wallace from 1299 to 1304, all took pains to see that bishops and abbots were appointed who would serve and support the community of the realm against foreign attack. And while the bishops and other clergy undoubtedly took sides or were partisan already by birth and environment, so that Fraser of St Andrews was pro-Balliol, Wishart of Glasgow pro-Bruce, nevertheless it is undeniable that the Scottish church as a whole maintained a consistently 'national' attitude and did much in its preaching and writing to propagate 'national' feeling. Bishop David of Moray taught his flock that there was as much merit in fighting the English as in warring against the infidel Saracens. In 1296 an obscure Edinburgh priest named Thomas solemnly 'excommunicated' King Edward I with bell and candle as he led his conquering army into the Scottish capital. The English and Scottish clergy of this period foreshadowed unmistakably the sharply nationalist divisions of the western church which became so familiar at the time of the Great Schism of 1378–1417 and at the Councils of the fifteenth century.

It is much harder to gauge the feelings of the common people, for they have left no poetry or chronicle and very little in the way of record. They did not form a single, still less a self-conscious class. As a general rule, servants looked to and followed the tenantry, tenants the gentry, gentry the nobles to whom they were bound by ties of employment, tenure, regions or kinship, or a mixture of these relationships. It would be wrong to think of the wars of independence as a struggle involving only the noble orders, save for the slaughter and destruction which certainly did not spare the poor and humble. When a well-informed contemporary such as Walter of Guisborough tells us that English invaders of Annandale in 1298 were attacked by the local peasantry and that 'the common people of the land' followed Wallace as their leader and ruler, it behoves us to take his words seriously. Again, John Barbour, whose report of personal names and similar details is so exact, was surely not writing fiction in his tale of the West Lothian small farmer ('husband') William Bunnok, 'a stout carle and a sture, and of him-self dour and hardy', who wrested the castle of Linlithgow from its English garrison by wedging in the gateway a waggon of hay crammed with armed countrymen. Episodes like this, however picturesque, do not tell us much, but there is a consideration of general importance to bear in mind when we are trying to assess the part played by the non-noble class. For centuries the Scots had been familiar with a universal obligation to perform military service, especially for the defence of their land in an emergency. The men who were thus called up, in earldom after earldom, equipped with spear and axe and bow, were not squires and knights and lairds but the ordinary adult male population of the burghs and countryside. For example, we are told that four husbandmen were the tenants of one plough-gate of land in Bowden, Roxburghshire, in 1327. They had to find one man equipped with armour who in turn would be the leader of 30 archers recruited from the barony of Bowden as its share of military service in 'the lord king's army'. It was thus that the common man would serve on occasions when 'the order was given for every man to go forth and defend his head'. Wallace and Bruce both made good use of the 'common army of Scotland'.

By the autumn of 1297 the English had been driven out of Scotland. The great rising led by Andrew Murray ('de Moray') in the north and by William Wallace in the south had produced an army which took the English administration by surprise and at Stirling Bridge on 11th September inflicted on its forces a defeat all the more crushing for being scarcely credible. Men on foot, largely unarmoured, did not beat knights in battle, nor Scots the English. Now both rules had been dramatically broken. Murray and Wallace, moreover, were young men, showing their elders how the community of Scotland should be led. Murray, who might have emerged as a brilliant military leader, died soon after the fight, probably from a fatal wound. For nine months Wallace was supreme, knighted by one of the leading earls (Strathearn?) and ruling as Guardian in the name of the wretched King John Balliol. Scots nobles taken to Flanders by Edward I hurried home to stiffen the national resistance, but they either would not or could not take the leadership from the popular champion. His test came at Falkirk on 22 July 1298, when he chose to fight an essentially defensive, static battle with his immovable infantry 'schiltroms' against Edward I's much more mobile and experienced force of cavalry, archers and slingers. Instead of being under the sluggardly leadership of the earl of Surrey, as at Stirling Bridge, the English army was led by King Edward in person, at the height of his career and prestige. When his Welsh auxiliaries threatened mutiny, his terse response was: 'We shall beat both the Welsh and the Scots in one day'. The Scots suffered a crushing defeat with heavy casualties, and Wallace, escaping with many of the other leading men from the field, was forced to yield his command to an aristocratic committee.

The outstanding personalities of Wallace and Bruce have always prevented us from seeing that the dark years from 1298 to 1306 were at least as important for the success of the Scottish struggle as the highlights of Stirling Bridge, Falkirk and Bannockburn. Two young noblemen, John Comyn (the 'Red Comyn') and Robert Bruce, came to the forefront. Comyn was son – soon to succeed his father – of the lord of Badenoch, chief of a powerful and ramifying baronial clan. Bruce (also soon to succeed his father, lord of Annandale) was in his own right earl of Carrick. He inherited the next best claim to the Scottish Crown after Balliol's. It was soon clear that they could not work in harness and in 1302 Bruce, ever mindful of his claim to the throne, deserted his former comrades still supporting Balliol and came over to Edward I. No less important at this stage than Comyn and Bruce were William Lamberton, bishop of St Andrews, John de Soulis, Simon Fraser, the chancellor Nicholas of Balmyle and the Bologna-trained Scots jurist Baldred Bisset, who prepared the Scottish case when the dispute with England was put before the papacy in 1301. Bisset emerges from these rather obscure years as a forensic champion of his country much as Wallace had emerged as its soldier champion. And Wallace himself was by no means *hors de combat*: he pleaded the Scots cause at the French and papal courts and after he returned to Scotland (1303?) he joined Fraser in some very effective guerilla warfare, of a kind which he perhaps ought to have concentrated on in 1298. Abandoned by their French allies and by the papacy, the Scots were overwhelmed by Edward I's last massive campaign against them in 1303–4. Comyn and other leaders surrendered on terms, Stirling Castle fell after a brutal siege, hundreds of prominent Scots were once again compelled to do homage to the English king and eventually, in the autumn of 1305, a new administration was set up, the basis of which was that Scotland was no longer a kingdom but merely a territory directly subject to the English crown – comparable perhaps to the present-day status of the Isle of Man and the Channel Isles. Before this had happened, Wallace, who had never submitted or acknowledged English overlordship, was captured and executed as a 'traitor' (24 August 1305). There were others, too, who refused to submit: John de Soulis among them, and probably a number of leading churchmen, for whom exile in France was the unavoidable lot.

Neither the settlement of 1305 nor the execution of Wallace had accomplished the conquest of Scotland. In February 1306, Bruce and his old rival Comyn met in the Greyfriars Kirk at Dumfries and quarrelled violently over a proposal that Bruce should be made king of Scots; in the quarrel Comyn was slain, and Bruce, with the obviously pre-arranged co-operation of the bishops of St Andrews and Glasgow, secured his hold over a number of vital south-country castles and was then (25 March) crowned at Scone. Almost at once he was worsted by an English counter-attack, and for nearly a year he skulked in hiding in Ireland and the Hebrides. Six months before Edward I died at Burgh on Sands in Cumberland (7 July 1307) Bruce returned to his own earldom of Carrick on the Scottish mainland. From this precarious base, employing a combination of enormous patience, reckless courage and ruthlessly savage guerilla attacks, Bruce built up a position of such strength that by late May he had beaten an English army in the field. Before the end of the year the English had abandoned much of their hold over Scotland, leaving Bruce free to concentrate on defeating his numerous and powerful internal enemies – especially the Comyns in the north-east and the central Highlands and the Macdougalls in Argyll. Rapid marches foreshadowing the campaigns of the great Montrose, brilliant surprise attacks and the systematic razing of captured castles showed that the new king was a military leader of genius. Despite a residue of doubt and bitterness arising from the supplanting of Balliol claims and the killing of the Red Comyn, the country rallied to Bruce as it had done to Wallace. And compared to Wallace, Bruce had three notable advantages : he was a crowned king, by an undoubted hereditary right; he possessed more versatility and skill as a general; and instead of confronting Edward, the 'Hammer of the Scots', at the height of his powers he had to deal with the insouciant, pleasure-loving Edward II, whose hostility towards the Scots though fierce enough in spirit was fitful in application.

The years from 1309 to 1313 were spent in retaking Scottish castles occupied by the English in 1306 and in carrying the war – in the shape of destructive, terrorizing raids – far into the north of England. Plunder was seized as far south as Beverley and Knaresborough, and large sums of 'blackmail' were levied from towns and country districts willing to pay heavily to avoid a visit from the

Scots. Although Edward II had some good commanders who knew Scotland well, men such as Aymer de Valence and Henry de Beaumont, the English were never able to regain the initiative in this period. Consequently, for them as much as for King Robert the year's respite given to the Stirling garrison in 1313 by his younger brother Edward Bruce posed an inescapable challenge to a battle which in the long run was likely to prove decisive. Had the English won, it is hard to see how the ancient Scottish monarchy could have survived, and though the Scottish nation might have done so it would not have become a 'nation-state' and its development over the following centuries would surely have followed a very different path from that which our history did in fact follow. A Scots victory, on the other hand, while it would not bring immediate peace or the terms which King Robert wanted would mean that the English kings had lost the initiative in Scotland for good.

All the same, Bannockburn (Sunday and Monday, 23–24 June, 1314), a full-scale pitched battle on confined ground against an enemy vastly superior in numbers, armour and weaponry, was the last kind of warfare that the Scots wanted. Its outcome, making every allowance for Edward II's poor generalship, was due to a genius for leadership and military tactics in Robert Bruce which long before his death had been recognised throughout Europe. There is no reason to believe that the Scots who bled with Wallace at Falkirk or were led at Halidon (1333) by Archibald Douglas or at Neville's Cross (1346) by King David II were less courageous or determined than their compatriots – in some cases the same individuals – who filled King Robert's schiltroms at Bannockburn. But 'Good King Robert', despite his chequered beginnings, possessed the magic of a commander who wins his battles. He knew exactly how best to seize on every weakness of an enemy, to be more highland than the highlanders when fighting on the slopes of Ben Cruachan yet, on more level terrain as at Bannockburn, to deploy his schiltroms aggressively as though they were moving human 'tanks' instead of keeping them fixed as Wallace had done.

Had Edward II been taken prisoner at Bannockburn a lasting peace would almost certainly have followed the battle, and papal and international recognition of King Robert's position would have been a matter of months, not years. As it was, Edward escaped, to lead or despatch armies against the Scots on several more occasions, but unable to prevent the Scots recovering Berwick, the last town in Scotland still in English hands, in 1318. It was nearly ten years after Bannockburn before Robert I was reconciled with the papacy, twelve years before he could renew the Franco-Scottish alliance of 1295–6, badly shaken by Philip IV's abandonment of the Scots in 1303, and it was almost fourteen years before an English King – by now the fifteen-year-old Edward III – and parliament could be persuaded to make what was intended to be a definitive, permanent peace. The Treaty of Edinburgh-Northampton (17 March 1328) annulled English claims to overlordship, recognised the Scottish kingdom under King Robert – with its boundaries as they had been in Alexander III's days – as 'separate, whole, free and in peace without subjection', provided for a marriage between the child David Bruce, King Robert's late-born son and heir, and young Joan of the Tower, Edward III's sister, and stipulated that the Scots should pay the English £20,000 'for the sake of peace'.

Robert I died, aged fifty-five, a year after peace had been made with England, surely with every reason to hope that this peace would be lasting and would bring back the fruitful harmony which had marked the relations between the two countries for most of the two centuries from 1093 to 1296. Despite the almost incessant warfare of much of his reign, King Robert was remembered not only as the champion, the Judas Maccabaeus, of his people but also as a humane and just ruler and strong lawgiver. When in 1320 the Scots barons addressed their famous letter to Pope John XXII (the 'Declaration of Arbroath') they acknowledged in memorable words the separate existence and character of 'this poor little Scotland, beyond which there is no dwelling-place', and in speaking of 'our laws and customs which we shall maintain unto death' and of the freedom of the kingdom which they would defend as long as one hundred remained alive, they were not only echoing words which had been used by the Treaty of Birgham, by Wallace, by Baldred Bisset and by the lairdly trio of Campbell, Hay and Seton; their phrases capture for us an instant in the evolution of the Scottish nation as it had been slowly but surely developing during the twelfth and thirteenth centuries. It was King Robert's grasp of the needs and true character of this feudal kingdom emerging into a national state which gave his reign lasting importance.

The legacy of Robert the Bruce may have been glorious, and doubtless it grew more glorious in retrospect. The actual situation in which Scotland found herself at his death was pregnant with disaster. The new king was a boy of five. Through his much older half-sister Marjorie, David II had a nephew eight years older than himself, Robert the Stewart, who would have become king in 1329 instead of 1371 had his uncle never been born. Despite the Stewart's undoubted shortcomings, it would surely have been better for Scotland to have had an adult ruler to cope with the dangers of the 1330s. John Balliol, who died in 1313, had left a son Edward. From his base in England, the younger Balliol almost at once made a bid for the throne with the help of a few nobles whom Robert I, for good reasons, had disinherited. The last of the great men of King Robert's heroic days, James lord of Douglas and Thomas Randolph earl of Moray, were dead, to be succeeded in the leadership of the community of the realm by an assortment of nobles many of whom were sadly inept and incompetent. In successive years, 1332 and 1333, two full-scale Scots armies were cut to pieces and their leaders slain by invading forces, respectively under Edward Balliol and Edward III in person, who showed ironically enough that they had learned and remembered more of the great Bruce's tactics than the Scots themselves. By rights, Dupplin Muir, after which Balliol had himself crowned king of Scots, and Halidon Hill, after which Edward III re-asserted an overlordship which his own solemn treaty of Edinburgh had disavowed, should have seen the total dismemberment of Scotland and consigned the struggles of Wallace and Bruce, Soulis and Lamberton, to oblivion. But the idea of the community of the realm was not forgotten. Five fortresses, Dumbarton, Lochleven, Kildrummy, Castle Urquhart on Loch Ness and Loch Doon in Galloway held out bravely against the invaders. The boy king was shipped to France in safety and installed at Château Gaillard, with the abbot of Kelso as his tutor and a handful of noblemen and bishops to form his court. At home Sir Andrew Murray of Bothwell, son of Wallace's colleague mortally wounded at Stirling Bridge, held the time-honoured place of Guardian, and painfully reverted to the Fabian guerilla tactics of King Robert's early years. In 1335 he inflicted a resounding defeat on Balliol's chief supporters in Scotland at the battle of Culblean in Aberdeenshire, and though he could not stop Edward

III twice more returning to invade the country the Scots under his and Robert Stewart's leadership had recovered their nerve and their strength so successfully by 1341 that it was thought safe to bring King David back home. By this time Edward III's ambitious energies had been diverted to France. A country which harboured his enemies could also be a rich source of plunder. The Scots historian Andrew Wyntoun has a good story to illustrate the mood of Scotland during this grim decade: no one dared resist the occupying Englishmen who were everywhere in strength; only the children, too young to choose between good and evil, when asked whose men they were answered 'richt apertly' they were King Davy's men –

> They knew no fear their mind to say
> for their king was a child as they.

The 40s and 50s were the nadir of 'King Davy's' long reign. After the French suffered the crushing defeat of Crécy (August 1346) Philip IV called on the Scots to fulfil the spirit of the Auld Alliance by invading England. In October, King David led his army in an ill-judged and impetuous raid south of the Tyne, and at Neville's Cross, outside Durham, the Scots were calamitously defeated. The king himself was captured, and his nephew the Stewart, whose conduct on the field of battle was regarded by English observers as frankly treacherous, fled safely back to Scotland to assume once more the position of Guardian. A crippling ransom was imposed for David II's release, and six years passed before the Scots king could even return briefly, on parole, to try to hasten the collection of the money, variously fixed at ninety or a hundred thousand merks (approximately £67,000), When in 1356 the Scots seemed to be back-pedalling on the deal, Edward III, with characteristic brutality, devastated the south-eastern counties in the 'Burnt Candlemas'.

David Bruce, perhaps not surprisingly, has had a bad press among historians. It is refreshing and salutary that recently his character and conduct have found some sympathetic defenders. Rather than compare him with his father it might be fairer to place him beside his Stewart successors down to James V, for the problems he had to face were more like their problems. Kingship faced new and severe challenges from the mid-fourteenth century. An uneasy baronage struggled to defend its old pre-eminence, the middle-class emerged with new strength, the whole of society was shaken by pestilence, a questioning of the customary forms of religious life, and agrarian and social upheavals. Yet kings, like other politicians, are judged by results. David II set an evil precedent when he allowed the Franco-Scottish alliance to push him into an ill-timed invasion of England, and the Scots under his own command suffered a disastrous defeat. The ransom which resulted had to be negotiated under the shadow of renewed English threats to Scottish independence. And, to complete a sorry chapter of failure, King David was unable to bequeath to his sorely-tried kingdom an heir of his own blood and lineage. The royal Bruces died with him.

ORKNEY and
SHETLAND
(NORWEGIAN)

CAITHNESS

SUTHERLAND

Dornoch △

Ross △
Elgin
□ Pluscarden
Inverness
Lochindorb ■
Harlaw
Kildrummy
Aberdeen △

THE LORDSHIP OF THE ISLES

Gasklune
Brechin △
Dunkeld △
Arbroath □
Lismore △
Scone □
Perth
Falkland ■
St. Andrews △
Dunblane
Doune ■ Lochleven □
Stirling ■
Bannockburn
The Bass Rock
Dumbarton ■
Falkirk
Linlithgow □
Tantallon ■
Nth.
Berwick
Dunbar
Rothesay ■
Glasgow △
Edinburgh ■
Nesbit Muir
Bothwell □
Newbattle □
Berwick upon Tweed
Melrose □
Homildon
Dryburgh □
Hill
Jedburgh □

Loch Doon ■

CARRICK
Lochmaben □
Lincluden □
Otterburn
Dumfries
Threave ■
Caerlaverock ■

Whithorn △

△ Cathedral
□ Abbey, Priory or
  Collegiate Church
■ Castle
● Burgh
✗ Battle

0 miles   50

0 kms   50   100

Fig 3 Medieval Scotland

CHAPTER II

Crown in Jeopardy

Ranald Nicholson

On 7 October 1357 David II returned to Scotland, a free man after almost eleven years of tedious captivity. Four days before, the treaty of Berwick had settled his ransom at 100,000 merks, to be paid in ten yearly instalments. As security twenty-three noble hostages were delivered to Edward III. When a council met at Scone on 6 November it ratified the treaty (which brought Scotland a much-needed truce) and made provision to meet the ransom instalments. The initial measures proved to be insufficient and had to be supplemented by the raising of the great customs levied on Scotland's chief exports – wool, fleeces and hides. In 1358 the rate of duty was doubled; in 1359 it was trebled; in 1368 it would be quadrupled, and the rate of £1.33p then levied on each sack of wool would remain constant until the sixteenth century. Thanks to various financial expedients the first ransom instalment was duly paid at midsummer 1358 and the second instalment was belatedly paid in 1359; but no further instalment would be paid until 1366.

This was hardly a result of insolvency: David rapidly brought order out of the financial chaos that had existed during the lieutenancy of the Steward. In 1362 the chamberlain (no great noble but a civil servant, Walter of Biggar) accounted for receipts of £7,380 and his account showed a surplus of £4,544; by 1363 the king had a deposit of 5,000 merks in Stirling Castle. But if David was able to pay his ransom he was not eager to do so. Despite the stringent conditions of the Treaty of Berwick he hoped to evade his obligations by assiduous diplomacy: in a number of visits to the English court he cultivated a special relationship with Edward III on the basis of their mutual interest in chivalry.

This, however, blinded neither side to national interest. By November 1363 Edward's patience was exhausted. From David he wanted more than fair words. At Westminster, where the two kings and their Privy Councils held negotiations, two memoranda were drafted. The first of these re-opened the question of the Scottish succession: Edward would make no demand for the residue of the ransom, would release the Scottish hostages and restore occupied territory on the Borders, provided that he were recognised as David's successor in the event of the latter's dying without legitimate offspring; if Edward thus became 'king of England and Scotland' he would undergo a second coronation at Scone and the separate identity and territorial integrity of Scotland would be carefully preserved. The second memorandum envisaged that a childless David might be succeeded by one of Edward's younger sons, in which case the English concessions would be fewer.

Edward's proposals had been ingeniously formulated. An alteration in the succession did not, in theory at least, diminish the independence of Scotland, which, according to the first memorandum, would have had the status that it came to possess after the union of the crowns in 1603; and David had little desire to preserve the succession for his heir presumptive, Robert the Steward, who had deserted him at Neville's Cross. Even so, David did not commit himself to accepting the proposals: playing for time he hoped that he might foil both Edward and the Steward by producing offspring of his own.

On 4 March 1364 parliament met to debate the Westminster memoranda. Some spoke in favour of the first of these, some in favour of the second, and the king does not appear to have influenced the discussions, though he may (for the sake of diplomacy) have given a show of annoyance when both memoranda were ultimately rejected and the Steward's position as heir presumptive was preserved.

No specific diplomatic crisis followed. Instead there was a sense of impending crisis for the next few years as parliaments and councils met in rapid succession to hear the reports from each embassy sent to England. Edward demanded impossible conditions for the peace or long truce that the Scots desired. The best that could be achieved was a second ransom treaty in May 1365, harsher than the first: it reduced the yearly ransom instalments to 6,000 merks (£4,000) but increased the total ransom to £100,000, and the truce was assured only until 2 February 1370, when either side might renew the war on six months' notice.

The situation changed in 1369 when France, having recovered from the disasters of the previous decades, re-opened hostilities with England. In June David went with a Scottish embassy to England

and came back with a third ransom treaty much more favourable to the Scots. The ransom was now set at the original figure of 100,000 merks and credit was given both for the 20,000 merks paid under the first treaty and the 24,000 paid under the second; the remaining 56,000 merks were to be paid at the rate of 4,000 a year for the next fourteen years, during which time the truce would continue. By June 1370 David was again in London; but despite his apparent friendship with Edward he had sent Sir Archibald Douglas, illegitimate son of Bruce's foremost knight, on a mission to the French court. Had David lived longer he might have taken even greater advantage of the revival of French power by playing off France against England.

As it was, the king's brinkmanship had been remarkably successful : despite the weakness of his diplomatic position he had paid only enough of his ransom to maintain the truce; at the same time he had extended his influence in the Borders, even over areas that the English still occupied; and at his death Scotland remained as independent as ever.

These achievements were accompanied by a striking restoration of royal authority. The council of November 1357 did not look in vain to the king 'to strike terror into wrongdoers'. He had come back to Scotland toughened by years of adversity and soon showed that he could rule with 'radure' (rigour), punishing 'mysdoaris' so that 'nane durst welle wythstand his will'.

First, reliable political support had to be enlisted against the great nobles who were ranged with the Steward in real or potential opposition. This support was forthcoming from talented knights such as Sir Robert Erskine and Sir Archibald Douglas 'the Grim', from churchmen such as William Landallis, bishop of St Andrews from 1342 to 1385 and Walter Wardlaw, archdeacon of Lothian and secretary to the king, who became bishop of Glasgow in 1367 and Scotland's first cardinal in 1383. Nor did David regard merchant burgesses such as John Mercer of Perth, Roger Hogg of Edinburgh and John Crabb of Aberdeen, merely as financial agents : they and their like wielded an economic power that merited political recognition. It was nothing new that the burghs were represented by commissioners in one council at Perth in January 1357, in another at Edinburgh in September, and in a third held by King David at Scone in November. What was new was the phrase *tres communitates* (three estates) which seems then

C

to have been used for the first time in Scotland. The old community of the realm had become a trinity in which the burgesses figured, alongside churchmen and barons, as a political entity, an 'estate' whose approval must be sought for any government measure that relied upon a consensus of opinion.

For a few years the king acted cautiously and showed no sign of antagonising the magnates : in 1357 the Steward was granted the earldom of Strathearn and in 1358 William Douglas was given the new title of earl of Douglas. A turning point came in 1360 when the king's mistress, Katherine Mortimer, was treacherously stabbed to death. The earl of Angus, suspected of having arranged the assassination, was imprisoned in Dumbarton castle, where he soon died of a fresh outbreak of plague. During this 'second mortality' of 1362 David moved north to seize Kildrummy Castle, the stronghold of the earl of Mar, who in 1359 had done homage to Edward III. A few months later, in January 1363, Robert the Steward rose in rebellion with his sons and allies. Complaining that money raised for the ransom was being squandered by 'evil counsel' they demanded that the king follow 'better counsel' – which would naturally be forthcoming from themselves rather than simple knights, churchmen and burgesses. But another issue was involved – the king's liaison with Dame Margaret Logie, daughter of Sir Malcolm Drummond and widow of Sir John Logie. David's queen had tactfully gone to England soon after he returned to Scotland, and her death in 1362 allowed him to contemplate marriage with Dame Margaret. If she bore him a child the Steward would lose his hopes of the crown.

In the crisis of 1363 the king did not waver; and among the rebels only the earl of Douglas showed fight. By April the 'great conspiracy' was over. At Inchmurdoch, a manor of the bishop of St Andrews, David celebrated his victory by marrying Dame Margaret and extracted from the Steward a sealed undertaking that 'I will be faithful for all the term of my life to . . . the Lord David, illustrious king of Scots'.

Towards the end of his reign David devoted himself to three tasks – improving the efficiency of government, strengthening the crown's economic position, and disciplining the great nobles. The three estates frequently met, usually at Scone or Perth, either in parliaments or in councils that were described as 'full' or 'general'. Increased use of parliamentary commissions and committees helped to streamline business, particularly the judicial business that came before parliament as the supreme court of law. The exchequer audits, which were held regularly at Perth, were often attended by the king, who used the constant question of the ransom as a pretext for the levying of contributions. These, towards the end of the reign, approximated to an annual income tax – and it was David, rather than the English, who received most of the proceeds. Between May and July 1366 a new assessment of landed rents was made throughout the kingdom. In the following year a parliamentary commission issued a sweeping act of revocation designed to restore to the crown all lands and revenues that had been alienated since 1329. It was not necessarily intended to put this act into full effect; but it gave the king a bargaining position in his dealings with the magnates, particularly Robert the Steward, his brother-in-law, William, earl of Ross, and his son-in-law, John, lord of the Isles.

John, greatest of the Gaelic chiefs, who dominated the Western Isles and had long pursued an independent course, had no desire to be subjected to firm royal control. He and his allies (with the exception of the cautious Steward) were usually 'contumaciously absent' from parliament. The reckoning came in the winter of 1369 when David visited Inverness : the lord of the Isles humbly begged pardon, delivered hostages, and undertook to pay taxes and obey royal officials. About the same time William, earl of Ross was forced to accept Sir Walter Leslie, one of the king's favourite knights, as son-in-law and eventual heir 'on account of the rigour of the same lord king'. Latterly no noble could offend the king (or queen) with impunity : the Steward and some of his sons were temporarily imprisoned in 1368; in 1369 he was deprived of his earldom of Strathearn for a few months; in 1370 the earl of Mar was a prisoner on the Bass Rock.

Only in Dame Margaret Logie did David meet his match. It was not her fault that she failed to produce an heir – she already had a son by her first husband while no child had blessed David's various liaisons. By 1369 he had been struck by the attractions and potential fecundity of Agnes Dunbar and assumed that Dame Margaret would be content with a pension of £100 'after the celebration of divorce'. Instead she took ship, made her way to the papal court, and appealed against her divorce; her charms won the kindly eye of pope and cardinals, and there was talk of placing

Scotland under interdict. The prospect of wearing a crown was revealed to Agnes Dunbar when she was granted a pension of 1,000 merks; a month later, on 22 February 1371, at the age of forty-six, King David unexpectedly died.

At the exchequer audit held a week before the king's death the chamberlain's account showed receipts of over £15,000, nearly all forthcoming from the great customs and direct taxation. Thanks to the ransom David II ended his reign in a stronger financial position than any other ruler of medieval Scotland. His own prosperity was matched by that of the merchant burgesses, who had brought the export trade to a peak that would not be surpassed until the sixteenth century. Sometimes capricious, but never cruel, David had taught the great nobles to respect royal authority.

These achievements soon withered away. It was symptomatic that at David's death the earl of Douglas made a bid for the throne and had to be mollified by concessions before the Steward could be crowned as Robert II. Likeable, but mediocre, the first Stewart king failed to rule his own family, let alone his kingdom. He had at least twenty-one offspring. Four, including Walter, earl of Atholl, were the children of his second marriage (with Euphemia of Ross) and had undoubtedly been born in lawful wedlock. Others, including the heir apparent, John, earl of Carrick, were the product of a previous marriage (with Elizabeth Mure) for which the necessary papal dispensation had been belatedly obtained. The obvious illegitimacy of the king's remaining sons and daughters did not prevent their expecting advancement. Through the marriages of his 'multitude of offspring' the whole nobility of Scotland was rapidly Stewartised; and those who were 'sib to the king' often stood above the law. Lacking the will to enforce the law Robert II did nothing in 1382 when his nephew, Sir James Lindsay of Crawford, murdered his son-in-law, John Lyon, thane of Glamis. In a general council of 1384 the three estates asserted that 'offences and outrageous crimes have been wont to be committed . . . for no short time' and appointed the earl of Carrick to restore law and order. By 1388 the heir apparent had shown his incapacity, and the king's second son, Robert, earl of Fife and Menteith, the only member of the royal family who displayed political talent, was appointed guardian of the realm.

Thanks to the lassitude of Robert II the Scots failed to win much profit from the favourable international situation. English reverses in France, together with the death of the redoubtable Edward III, allowed them to stop further payment of David II's ransom. But although the troubles of England during the minority of Richard II invited a Scottish offensive on the Borders this was pursued aimlessly: the initiative came not from the crown but from Border magnates who were inspired less by nationalism than by the quest for booty and chivalric renown. On 2 February 1384, the truce, often broken, was not renewed; the surrender of Lochmaben ended the English occupation of Annandale but was followed by a punitive expedition during which John of Gaunt, duke of Lancaster, held Edinburgh to ransom. Nor did much result from the renewal of the Franco-Scottish alliance in 1371, even although an ambitious scheme was devised for a joint attack upon England in the summer of 1385: the French would land in the south while the Scots invaded in the north. Jean de Vienne, admiral of France, arrived in Scotland with over a thousand men-at-arms and 50,000 gold francs, which were distributed to the more bellicose Scottish nobles. But there was no French invasion of southern England, and the Franco-Scottish expedition which set out for the Borders in July merely brought another English punitive expedition under Lancaster and the young Richard II. This time Edinburgh was burnt, together with the abbeys of Melrose, Dryburgh and Newbattle.

There followed a number of short truces until the Scots took advantage of fresh English dissensions to mount two simultaneous raids in the summer of 1388. One raid, upon Cumberland, brought booty. The other, upon Northumberland, brought chivalric glory as well. At Otterburn, on 5 August, Henry Hotspur, son and heir of the earl of Northumberland, was made prisoner. Although the victor, James, earl of Douglas, was slain in the fight, he achieved immortality in the dying speech attributed to him by the chronicler Froissart, whose tales made the aristocracy of Europe well aware of the knightly prowess (and barbarous poverty) of the Scots.

The death of the second earl of Douglas at Otterburn had important consequences within Scotland. The succession to most of his lands was laid down in a tailzie (entail) of 1342, of which Archibald the Grim was the sole surviving beneficiary. In 1369 David II had granted him the lordship of eastern Galloway; in

1372 he had bought western Galloway and re-united the distinctive province that had been divided in the previous century. As principal heir of the victor of Otterburn Archibald now became third earl of Douglas and acquired Douglasdale, Eskdale, Lauderdale, and the lucrative forest of Selkirk. His towerhouse of Threave established a new and austere fashion in baronial architecture, just as his foundation of collegiate churches at Lincluden and Bothwell established a new fashion in ecclesiastical development. His firmness and justice in administering his lands, together with his prowess in warfare, stood out in sharp contrast to the maladministration and lack of spirit of Stewart kingship. When Robert II died on 19 April 1390 the house of Douglas dominated southern Scotland.

The earl of Carrick, who now became king at the age of fifty-three, changed his name of John (then thought unlucky) and reigned as Robert III. But fortune was not to be cheated: one of the new king's brothers, Alexander Stewart, earl of Buchan, popularly known as the Wolf of Badenoch, had long been at feud with the aged bishop of Moray; on 17 June 1390, two months before the coronation of Robert III, the Wolf emerged from his fastness at Lochindorb with a band of 'wyld wykkyd Helandmen' and burnt the cathedral of Elgin. His royal blood protected him from undue criticism.

The burning of Elgin was followed by further trouble in the north-east and central Highlands. In 1392 a troop of Highland caterans mauled the chivalry of Angus at Gasklune. In 1396, in an effort to compose the differences between two feuding clans, a trial by battle on the grand scale was held on the North Inch of Perth. The king presided while 'thre score wyld Scottis men', thirty from each clan, fought in mortal combat. When he cast down his baton to end the conflict only a dozen survived. Disorder continued. The chronicler of Moray, inspired by the wording of a statute of 1397 that vainly devised new procedures for the apprehension of criminals, despondently wrote of the state of affairs in 1398:

In those days there was no law in Scotland, but he who was stronger oppressed him who was weaker, and the whole realm was a den of thieves; murders, herschips and fire-raising, and all other misdeeds, remained unpunished; and justice, as if outlawed, lay in exile outwith the bounds of the kingdom.

These were days when Scottish knights were winning renown in English tournaments, attracted by the liberality of Richard II, who had no desire to continue warfare with the Scots. Liberality was also manifested by Robert III, who, since he could not dominate the nobles, tried to quieten them with gifts of cash, remissions of customs duty, life pensions and heritable pensions. The last were sometimes combined with a bond of retinue by which the recipient was contracted to serve the king or his son and heir, David, earl of Carrick. For their own defensive or offensive purposes the nobles resorted to similar devices: in a general council of 1399 it was hopefully enacted that all the king's lieges were to uphold the authority of his lieutenant notwithstanding 'ony condiciouns of retenewis'.

The person appointed to the new post of king's lieutenant was the heir apparent, who in 1398 had been raised to the dignity of duke of Rothesay at the same time as his uncle, Robert Stewart, earl of Fife and Menteith, had been created duke of Albany. Scotland's first dukes were soon engaged in a power struggle while Robert III stood helplessly aside. In a general council of January 1399 the king had been blamed for the misgovernance of the realm, and it was thought 'expedient' that his son and heir be appointed royal lieutenant for three years. In practice this meant that Albany was ousted from a dominant position in government. He was still powerful enough to see that his nephew's authority was restricted by twenty-one councillors appointed by the three estates. The council included only one burgess and was probably divided by the rivalries of the two ducal factions. Nor was the capricious Rothesay the man to compose differences: in 1400 he jilted the daughter of the earl of March in order to marry the daughter of Archibald the Grim, and the insulted earl absconded to the English court. When Rothesay refused to give up office at the end of his three-year term the king was persuaded to allow his arrest. On 26 March 1402 the heir apparent died in Albany's castle of Falkland of dysentery or of starvation. In a general council held in May lengthy debates and interrogations resulted in the conclusion that Rothesay had 'departed this life by divine providence and not otherwise'. Having won the power struggle Albany succeeded Rothesay as royal lieutenant.

But between Albany and the crown stood the figure of the king's remaining son, James. With some forethought Robert III decided to send the boy to France. He was escorted to North Berwick by Sir David Fleming, who was waylaid and slain on his return journey. For a month James lingered among the gannets of the Bass Rock before the *Maryenknyght* of Danzig called to take him aboard. When the vessel was off Flamborough Head on 22 March 1406 it was seized by English pirates and James was lodged in the Tower of London. On 4 April, a few days after he had received the news of his son's capture, Robert III died. He had once told his queen: 'Bury me, I pray, in a midden, and write for my epitaph "Here lies the worst of kings and the most wretched of men in the whole realm".'

Although the three estates recognised Robert III's son as James I, his youth and captivity necessitated the fullest delegation of royal functions. Albany, now heir presumptive, was appointed governor of the realm and assumed most of the trappings of kingship during a period when the relationship between Scotland and England was chaotic, but hardly dangerous. Possession of the person of James I gave the English a diplomatic advantage in their dealings with the Scots. The latter had been shocked by the deposition of Richard II in 1399 and were inclined to regard his successor, Henry IV, as a usurper. Although Henry had led an army to Edinburgh in August 1400 he had behaved with unique restraint, hoping to reach a peace settlement. But since he was not prepared to abandon the pretensions of his predecessors all that could be achieved was a series of truces, often interspersed with piracy at sea and affrays on the Borders. One of these, at Nesbit Muir on 22 June 1402, had ended with the capture of 'the flower of the chivalry of a great part of Lothian': in another at Homildon Hill on 14 September 1402 'the flower of chivalry of the whole realm of Scotland was captured and held to ransom'. Among the captives was Albany's son and heir, Murdoch Stewart. For many years there would be abortive negotiations for the ransom and release of Murdoch and James I. The only national advantage that was gained during this period was the recovery of Jedburgh in 1409; and this was the achievement not of Albany, or the nobles, but of 'mediocre persons of Teviotdale'.

Soon Albany's attention was distracted from Border warfare by a crisis in the north. When Alexander Leslie, earl of Ross, had died in 1402, he left his young daughter, Euphemia, as heiress to his earldom, and Albany (her grandfather) had assumed her wardship.

By 1411 he was trying, in devious fashion, to obtain her earldom for his second son, John, already earl of Buchan. Albany's moves antagonised his nephew, Donald, lord of the Isles, whose wife, Margaret (or Mary) Leslie, had contingent claims upon Ross.

Although half Stewart by birth, Donald represented the independent traditions of the MacDonalds of Islay, not those of the royal house. He was no mere leader of Highland caterans. His lordship of the Isles, organised partly in feudal fashion, was virtually autonomous – in 1408 there were negotiations for a league of perpetual peace and friendship between the lord of the Isles, Henry IV, and their subjects. It was a time when there was a growing realisation of the differences between the English-speaking Lowlanders and the Gaelic-speaking Highlanders and Islesmen (half the population of Scotland), whom the chronicler John of Fordun described as 'Wild Scots'. Although the latter were no more clannish than their Lowland contemporaries they were more influenced by continued contact with Gaelic Ireland than by the cosmopolitan institutions that in the last three centuries had transformed the Lowlands; their archaic way of life was proudly idealised by the bards; and the lord of the Isles, descendant of the illustrious Somerled, was the one man who might unite them all.

In 1411, in an attempt to foil Albany's designs upon the earldom of Ross, he seized Inverness and marched towards Aberdeen. His object of assuming control over the lands that belonged to the earldom of Ross was not incompatible with higher ambitions. At Harlaw, some twenty miles from Aberdeen, he engaged in battle on 24 July with his cousin, Alexander Stewart, earl of Mar. Then, and for long afterwards, this bloody encounter was regarded as a contest between Highlanders and Lowlanders. Just as the battle was inconclusive so also were the results: the Gaelic regions were no longer likely to be easily assimilated into Lowland Scotland; but the government, increasingly associated with the Lowlands, lacked the strength for an outright attack upon Gaelic culture and the separatist tendencies of the lordship of the Isles.

In any case attention was soon drawn to a renewed conflict between England and France: in 1415 Henry V bid fair to emulate Edward III's exploits by defeating a vast French army at Agincourt. In a bid to secure Scottish neutrality he accepted a ransom of £10,000 for Murdoch Stewart in 1416. But this did not have the desired effect : in October 1419 a Scottish expeditionary force under the earl of Buchan landed at La Rochelle to aid the dauphin. On 22 March 1421 the dauphin's troops and their Scottish allies defeated an English force at Baugé; although the Scots were on the losing side at Cravant on 31 July 1423 they had demonstrated that the English were not invincible.

Meanwhile the octogenarian Albany had died on 3 September 1420. Had he been king, rather than merely the power behind the throne, he might have made a good ruler – there can be no doubt that he was astute enough to win popularity. But he lacked the prestige that kingship would have conferred and was always forced to come to terms with the great nobles, as in 1409 when he concluded a bond of alliance with Archibald the Tyneman, fourth earl of Douglas. The chronicler Bower significantly remarked that 'if any enormities perchance were committed in the realm by the powerful he [Albany] patiently temporised, knowing how to reform them prudently enough at an opportune time'. The opportune time – his own accession to the throne – never came. But Albany was suspected of having done little to obtain the release of James I, and when the duke died it was his son, Murdoch, who stepped into his shoes as heir presumptive, second duke of Albany and governor of Scotland. What had eluded the father might not elude the son.

This prospect was distasteful to some nobles. Moreover Duke Murdoch lacked the political talent of his father and failed to keep his own sons under control. During his governorship the waning of central power was complete. This was particularly evident in the finances of government. The direct taxation so prudently introduced under the cover of David II's ransom had long been allowed to lapse. By 1418 the gross receipts from the great customs were scarcely £3,000 – only one third as much as in 1371. Little enough of the proceeds reached the government : between 1409 and 1420 Archibald the Tyneman seized about £5,000 from the customs officials of Edinburgh; and in 1420 his henchmen had seized their records lest they be produced in audit. The exchequer audit of 1422 showed that arrears of almost £4,000 were owing to the governor. The finances of central government had collapsed and it had been demonstrated that there was no substitute for a masterful king.

While there was a growing demand in Scotland for the return

of James I it was also thought in England that his release might be opportune. A move in this direction had been contemplated by the late Henry V, who had induced James to serve him in France in return for the chance of a trip to Scotland on parole. But nothing resulted until James attracted the interest of the powerful family of Beaufort, of royal, but illegitimate, descent. Its members were anxious to obtain royal connections and were well aware that the poet king had detected in the Lady Joan Beaufort 'beautee eneuch to mak a world to dote'. On 4 December 1423 a treaty for James's release was sealed at London. He could not be held to ransom since he was no prisoner of war, but £40,000 (60,000 merks) were to be paid in yearly instalments of 10,000 merks to cover the 'expenses' of his long residence in England. Already it was assumed that 10,000 merks would be remitted as dowry of the Lady Joan, whom James married in February 1424. In the following month the pair were at Durham, where final negotiations included the sealing of an indenture for a seven-year truce. While James and his bride arrived in Scotland at the beginning of April a concourse of Scottish nobles headed southward from Durham to act as hostages.

On his return James faced a sorry state of affairs. Since the accession of the first Stewart king there had been a progressive decline in the authority of central government, in its finances, in the export trade, but most of all in law and order. Although the consequent sufferings of the common people are seldom revealed in any detail their extent may be inferred from the frequent enactments of the three estates which testified to a wholesale collapse in respect for the law. Occasionally this was demonstrated in some violent crime that attracted the attention of the chroniclers since it took place within the ranks of the nobility. In 1402 Sir Malcolm Drummond, brother-in-law of Robert III, died in the prison of some assailant, possibly Alexander Stewart, illegitimate son of the Wolf of Badenoch; it was certainly in curious circumstances that Alexander married Sir Malcolm's widow and thereby obtained her earldom of Mar. In 1413 Patrick Graham, earl of Strathearn, was slain by Sir John Drummond, with whom he had lately concluded a bond of alliance.

Disorder of a different type – in the shape of heresy – simultaneously troubled the church. In 1406 or 1407 Master Laurence of Lindores, inquisitor of heretical pravity, condemned James

Resby, an English Lollard, and consigned him and his writings to the flames. Nonetheless in 1410 Quintin Folkhyrde, a Scottish esquire, zealously expressed radical views in the 'News from Scotland' that he sent to Prague, the centre of continental heresy.

Criticism of the church had been partly inspired by the consequences of the centralisation (sometimes bungling and always costly) that had taken place during the residence of the papacy at Avignon between 1309 and 1377. Increasingly the pope controlled the greater appointments in the church; increasingly they were hedged about with financial and political considerations. The situation worsened (and criticism increased) when the return of the papacy to Rome was followed in 1378 by the disputed papal election that brought on the Great Schism. Until this was healed by a general council of the church that met at Constanz from 1414 to 1417 there would be two popes (eventually three) – one at Rome, a second at Avignon, and a third elected at Pisa in 1409. The troubles of the Scottish monarchy coincided with those of the papacy just as the restoration of royal authority by James I would coincide with the restoration of papal authority by Martin V.

It would be wrong, however, to convey too grim an impression of early Stewart Scotland. Although there was a withering of central authority this did not necessarily lead to anarchy within each of the baronial or clannish communities that bounded the horizons of most of the population. In contrast to France and England there were no peasant risings in Scotland. On his own lands, among his own kinsmen and dependants, the great noble was a patriarch rather than a robber baron. His devotion to chivalry was no quixotic idiosyncrasy but a way of life that was taken for granted and earned him popularity. Nor was he uninterested in economic matters: he controlled land, by far the chief source of wealth; and in days when the merchant burgesses were hampered by various economic restrictions, sometimes self-imposed, only the chivalric noble was an uninhibited free agent. His 'crusading' ventures with the Teutonic Knights opened the Baltic to Scottish trade; the first Sinclair earl of Orkney crossed the Atlantic c. 1390 (though he found nothing that was considered rewarding); and the exploits of Scottish knights in France won for all classes of their compatriots the opportunities for advancement that were available in that rich land – when Joan of Arc triumphantly entered Orleans in 1429 the bishop who welcomed her was a Scotsman.

Moreover even during the Great Schism there were aspects of ecclesiastical life that were positive as well as those that were negative. Noble birth and financial backing were seldom by themselves a qualification for an important benefice unless they were supplemented by a university degree, especially one in canon or civil law. Benedict XIII, driven from Avignon to a citadel in Aragon, and grateful for the continuing support of the Scots, gave in 1413 the necessary confirmation to Bishop Wardlaw's foundation of Scotland's first university at St Andrews. Also, since England adhered to the Roman popes while Scotland recognised the Avignonese, the ecclesiastical conflict acquired patriotic overtones – Thomas Rossy, bishop of Galloway, even challenged the bishop of Norwich to mortal combat.

Patriotism, almost inextricably intermingled with an interest in chivalry, was a prominent characteristic of the literature of the period, most of it the work of ecclesiastics. In 1375 Archdeacon Barbour of Aberdeen produced his epic poem, *The Bruce*, written in the English dialect that had replaced French as the language of the Lowland aristocracy. Some ten years later, John of Fordun, a chantry priest of Aberdeen, composed a Latin chronicle which flatteringly traced the origins of the Scots to Scota, daughter of the pharaoh overwhelmed in the Red Sea, and thus showed that the Scots were not derived from the mythical Trojan heroes whom the English claimed as forbears. Shortly afterwards Thomas Barry, canon of Glasgow, celebrated the Scottish victory at Otterburn in spirited Latin verse. The *Orygenale Cronykil* compiled sometime between 1420 and 1424 by Andrew of Wyntoun, prior of Lochleven, was equally bad both as poetry and history but deliberately sought to inculcate loyalty, patriotism and virtue. If patriotism had found little practical expression in the Scotland of the early Stewarts, and had not been harnessed to national advantage, it had at least matured as a prevailing sentiment in the minds of the Scots.

CHAPTER III

Taming the Magnates?

Jennifer M. Brown

The period 1424–88 is not a particularly well known one. Traditionally it has been written off as one of the most lawless in Scottish history, and for that reason one of the least interesting. Only a few incidents stand out as familiar, and these are, without exception, cases of conflict between king and magnates : the murder of James I, the struggle between James II and the Black Douglases, the crises at Lauder where James III's favourites were hanged by a dissident nobility and Sauchieburn where James was killed. The traditional interpretation is that this was a period which saw a power struggle in which one or other side sometimes gained the upper hand, but which neither side actually won. The puzzle is why this should have been so. Why should the magnates of the fifteenth century, unlike their predecessors of, say, the twelfth and thirteenth centuries, have apparently moved into direct and open opposition to the monarchy? A possible explanation, which has been put forward for the whole of northern Europe, is that this century saw the decline of 'medieval' ideas in both church and state, that this was a society in its last decadent stages, about to give way to the new ideas of the modern world. Applied to Scotland, this would explain the traditional idea that the overmighty nobility who fought and killed James III in 1488 became the rather more civilised and co-operative magnates under the Renaissance king James IV. Another possibility, however, is that there is no good answer to the question of why there was conflict between crown and nobility because there was no such conflict. Rather, there were two ruthless, tough and unscrupulous kings who were very powerful indeed, and who hounded out the two greatest magnate families of the early fifteenth century; and a third king who failed to govern effectively, and who provoked a minor and limited rebellion which, remarkably, succeeded.

One major problem about the fifteenth century is the serious lack of reliable contemporary sources, both record and chronicle. Historians turn with relief to the reign of James IV simply because so much more information is available; the daily life of the king, for example, can be described in a way which is not possible for earlier monarchs because the Treasurer's Accounts, which give a wealth of detail, have survived continuously after 1488 but for only one year before that date. Much of our information about the fifteenth century, and in particular its crises, has therefore been drawn from the writings of sixteenth century chroniclers, the best known of which is the racy, entertaining and almost wholly unreliable history by Robert Lindsay of Pitscottie, produced in 1579. Recent research has shown that the traditional and previously accepted account of James III as the king who antagonised his nobility because of his dependence on lowborn favourites, the mason, the tailor, the musician, is a legend developed by sixteenth century writers without any contemporary justification. Likewise the Black Douglases, who dominated the early years of James II's personal rule, emerge as opponents of royal authority on the grand scale in Pitscottie's story; but one of his main examples of their over-mighty defiance is as much invention as his account of James III, for it turns on their illegal execution of one Thomas Maclellan, tutor of Bombie, a man for whose existence there is no evidence at all.

If the details which have gone into the building up of the idea of the overmighty nobility are suspect, the idea itself contains inexplicable paradoxes. While two of the kings of this period died violent deaths at the hands of their subjects, there remains the impressive fact that the ruling house survived unchallenged in spite of its problems and misfortunes. This in itself may seem a weak enough statement. But it is put into context when it is contrasted with the situation in England where the crown changed hands by violence six times between 1399 and 1485. In Scotland, the possibility that the legitimacy of the descendants of the first marriage of Robert II might be disputed has been used as the basis of the idea that the descendants of the second marriage entertained dynastic ambitions; it has been suggested that these ambitions lay behind the murder of James I, and also had their part in the Douglases' opposition to James II. Such an interpretation seems highly dubious, however, because it rests on the assumption that the descendants of the second marriage let their claim lie between 1390 and 1424 when the government was at its most vulnerable, and chose to press it in 1437 against a strong and effective king, having failed to take the elementary step of securing the person of the heir to the throne; and the actions of the Douglases after the murder of the eighth earl in 1452, while provocative enough, do not bear out the idea of a genuine dynastic attempt. In fact there was only one undoubted usurpation attempt in fifteenth century Scotland, that of James III's ambitious and totally irresponsible brother Alexander duke of Albany; and the most significant feature of that attempt was that Alexander found no support in Scotland, in spite of the obvious deficiencies of the king, a situation very different from that in England, where men were amazingly willing to support rebellions, however slight their chances of success. Moreover, as English experience showed, support for a usurper might bring appreciable reward if the rebellion was successful. Here was an opportunity for self-interested advancement for the 'overmighty' Scottish magnates. Yet they made no use of it.

There were also the opportunities offered by the appalling problem of the recurrent royal minorities, a problem which, while bad enough in the intermittent form in which it appeared in other countries, amounted to staggering proportions in Scotland where in the period 1406–88 there was no adult ruler for thirty-eight years. Yet with a few exceptions, these opportunities were not exploited; only four families – the Douglases, Livingstones and Crichtons in the 1440s, the Boyds of Kilmarnock in the 1460s – turned the situation to their advantage. In this century, the nobility had an unparalleled chance of self-aggrandizement at the expense of the crown. That they let it go is strong evidence of the position of prestige and respect which the fifteenth-century monarchy enjoyed, a position which is completely at odds with the idea of the 'overmighty nobility'. Indeed, so self-confident were these kings that they felt it unnecessary to resort to the usual pursuit of monarchs of surrounding themselves with a mystique based on a mythical line of ancestors, bolstered up by signs of unusual saintly or divine favour; the use of the name 'Jacobus Seneschallus' – James the Steward – shows how unconcerned they were to obscure the fact that their origins were neither mythical nor divine.

In terms of the traditional concept, it is curious that 'the nobility' did not challenge the crown; it is also curious that the crown did not challenge 'the nobility'. One problem about the traditional view is in fact a problem of terminology. There is an obvious convenience in referring to 'the nobility' rather than to 'a few of . . .' or 'some of the nobility'; the trouble is that one begins to believe it. But the phrase is seriously misleading in two ways. It suggests that the nobility as a class was regarded by the crown as a threat and a danger; and this is manifestly untrue. It also suggests a static group, and obscures the fact that there was a major change in both personnel and titles by the mid-fifteenth century; the paradox here is that the crown which was apparently threatened by the nobility managed to rid itself, partly by its own efforts, of many of them, and then proceeded to create the problem anew by replenishing the ranks.

The factors which produced this change show the idea of 'taming the magnates' to be an oversimplification, indeed a gross understatement when applied to the policy of James I; annihilating might be a better word. In 1424 there were fifteen earldoms (excluding the earldom of Orkney) and one dukedom. In 1437 when James died the dukedom had gone, and the earldoms were reduced to eight. The revenues of one of these was in the hands of the crown; one was held by a woman, the daughter of James I; two earls were in England as hostages; and only four remained with the families who had held them in 1424. The other seven had all fallen to the crown, either because of forfeiture or because of the failure of direct heirs, that situation which was potentially dangerous for any medieval landowning family and which became actually disastrous with a king as acquisitive and unscrupulous as James I.

James returned from England in 1424. He was a complex personality, an accomplished poet and good family man, vigorous, extremely efficient, and vindictive. The vigour and efficiency at once showed themselves in the flood of legislation poured out by his first three parliaments, the first of which was held in the minimum possible time after his return; in his attempts to reform parliament on English lines, which were unsuccessful; and in his rather more successful attempts to make administration more effective. His vindictiveness, which was understandable enough after eighteen years enforced absence in England, but at the same time repellent in its cold and calculating quality, was less immediately apparent. James waited for a year, during which he seems to have been on good enough terms with the former governor, Murdoch duke of Albany, who had negotiated James' return and

D

created no problems for the king when relinquishing his office. Then, entirely unexpectedly, James turned with great savagery on Murdoch, the two sons of Murdoch on whom he could get his hands, and, worst of all, Duncan earl of Lennox, an old man of about eighty whose only crime, apparently, was that of being Murdoch's father-in-law; in May 1425, they were all tried and executed at Stirling. James' delay of a year may be explained on the grounds that he was consolidating his position before taking such drastic action; the action itself is much more difficult to explain in any terms other than those of personal and unrelenting animosity reinforced by greed – because the windfall from the wholesale destruction of the Albany family, the earldoms of Fife and Menteith and the revenues of Lennox, was of course considerable.

The same personal vindictiveness showed itself again in the treatment of Malise Graham, earl of Strathearn. Graham, a descendant of Robert II's second marriage, not only lost his earldom, but was sent to England in 1427 as a hostage, and remained there until 1453, with only the less valuable earldom of Menteith as compensation. The sending of hostages to England, as security for his unpaid ransom, was used by James on other occasions as a convenient device. Most hostages remained in England for short periods, of one, three or five years. Graham was a notable exception; David, master of Atholl, son of the last surviving son of Robert II, was sent south in 1424 and died there in 1434; and John, earl of Sutherland was in England from 1427 until 1444, or possibly 1448. And acquisitiveness lay behind the king's contention that the earldom of Ross had lapsed to the crown after the death of John Strewart, earl of Buchan and Ross, in 1424; and the exclusion of the Erskine claimant to the earldom of Mar after the death of Alexander Stewart, earl of Mar, in 1435.

The greed and vindictiveness of James I can be amply demonstrated. The question remains whether his treatment of these magnates can be explained simply in these terms, or whether, as with his re-organisation of financial administration, greed and a genuine desire for more effective royal government intermingled to produce a consistent policy. Did James, in other words, regard it as essential to 'tame' the magnates? That such was his intention has been suggested as the motive behind the act of 1428 which attempted to bring the lairds as shire representatives to parliament, thus introducing an equivalent to the English house of Commons. Here is a clear example of the influence of his English experience. Yes – but one cannot be selective about the English influence, and argue that James saw the introduction of a lower house as a means of counteracting magnate power when his English experience must have shown him not only the advantages, as he saw them, of the English parliament, but also the fact that the Commons in England were by no means consistent supporters of the monarchy against the lords, and indeed sometimes acted in the reverse role. In any case, the lairds depended on the magnates, and this was not necessarily an anti-social force, but one which medieval kings used to their advantage. What James wanted in his attempted reforms can be seen in his legislation of 1426 which demanded that acts of parliament should be registered and circulated through-out the country that all might know his laws; in that year, he himself complained about and tried to legislate against absenteeism on the part of the magnates. The legislation of 1428 was an extension of his desire to ensure that parliament was more repre-sentative, and that its legislation was everywhere known; hence the lairds should be brought in, both to take part in the work of parliament, and to transmit it back to the localities.

The legislation of James' first three parliaments has similarly been seen as a reaction to a special situation in which, freed from control by the king, the irresponsible and overmighty magnates had increased the extent of lawlessness in Scotland. To a limited degree, this was true, but only in respect of certain individual nobles, and for the period before 1400 rather than after. The great theme of the first years of James' reign, justice for rich and poor alike, is not peculiar to this period. 'The pur comownis' appear time and again in parliamentary legislation of the fifteenth and sixteenth centuries. Concern for the lower classes had no doubt a certain propaganda value; but it was a genuine enough reflection of a fundamental social tenet of medieval society, the protection by the great of the lesser men who depended on them. James' legislation, therefore, did not consist of exceptional measures for an exceptional situation.

What was exceptional was the nature of the nobility; and it is this, along with his own unpleasant characteristics, which explains James' actions. In the period 1371–1424, the extensive family of

Robert II had so successfully cornered the market that in 1424 eight of the fifteen earldoms were held by Stewarts. What James quite clearly embarked on was a family vendetta. Thus the Albany family were exterminated; Malise Graham lost his earldom and his freedom. But the lord of the Isles, a greater trouble-maker than any Stewart in this reign, was merely temporarily imprisoned. And the most notable example of all was the earl of Douglas. The greatest heights of Douglas power were not reached until the minority of James II. But the earl of Douglas under James I was nonetheless a man of great power and influence; and if James indeed had a policy of 'taming the magnates' as a class, then his inaction against Douglas, apart from imprisoning him briefly in 1431, apparently because of suspected dealings with England, was an aberration totally unbelievable in a man of James' ruthless intelligence and efficiency. There are exceptions to this general view; to one Stewart, Walter, earl of Atholl, James showed no animosity, though in 1437 this did not pay off. But on the whole, the most consistent explanation of James' attitude is that he was determined to 'tame' not the nobility but the Stewart nobility; and so successfully did he do so that in the minority of James II the only Stewart earl left was Malise Graham, in England.

It has already been said that there is no evidence that any of the Stewarts had dynastic ambitions. But James clearly felt hemmed in by too many magnates close in blood to the crown, and regarded attack as the best form of defence. Why should he have felt this? In general, such a concentration of power in the state was a potential danger. And possibly James' English experience, which influenced his ideas on government, and his ideas on the burning of heretics, also influenced him here and heightened his concern; he had seen that English rebels readily found support, and he may not have felt inclined to wait for the situation to arise in Scotland. In the event, the family vendetta which he had begun was taken up by the other side, not to overthrow his line, but to remove a tyrant. When the final crisis came, even Atholl, the one Stewart who had not suffered under James, joined those who had; and James was murdered by a small and unrepresentative group of people, engaged not in a power struggle between crown and nobility, but in a family feud.

The depletion of the magnate class by 1437 cleared the way for the spectacular rise to power in the minority of James II of the lesser families of Livingstone and Crichton. It also threw into sharp relief the growing power of the Douglases. By 1449 there were eight earls in Scotland; three of them – Douglas, Ormond and Moray – were Douglas brothers, whose lands gave them powerful areas of influence both in the south-west, centred round their massive stronghold of Threave near Castle Douglas, and in the north. Again there was a concentration of power which the crown might well view with alarm. Beyond that, it is impossible to show any real threat by the Douglases. Only in the rationalisation of events found in later accounts is there any real suggestion that they were abusing the power they had. And the idea that James II brought them down because of their treasonable dealings with England can be demonstrated only after James' murder of earl William in 1452. It cannot be substantiated before then, for the evidence is simply not available; indeed, apart from the episode in the reign of James I, the Douglases had a long tradition of friendship with France, to the extent that the fourth and fifth earls had held French titles, the fourth being killed at Verneuil in 1424 while fighting for the French against the English. Open provocation first came not from the Douglases but from the king. In 1450–51, while the earl was abroad, James took over his lands of the earldom of Wigtown, and built up as a rival family in the south-west the Kennedies of Dunure. What the Douglases apparently wanted was to be left to enjoy their vast possessions. The crown's inroads into these possessions sparked off the chain of events and worsening relations which led to the famous murder of February 1452. This murder left James in a highly vulnerable position; and he survived only because most of the magnates, once again failing to take advantage of an opportunity to fulfil the role ascribed to them of opposing the crown, supported the king against the Douglases, to the extent that when the final conflict came in 1455, the Douglases were left entirely without allies, and easily defeated. It was a curious, dangerous affair. It is impossible to prove that the king's actions were justified, to be sure that the Douglases were an actual rather than a potential threat. But the parallel between James II and his father, the ruthlessness with which they reacted to a potential threat seems fairly close. And not only ruthlessness. The acquisitiveness of James I is seen again in James II's unscrupulous annexation of the earldom of Moray when direct male heirs had failed, and his exclusion of the Erskine claimant to the earldom of Mar; and it may well have been a large part of his attitude to the Douglases.

The crisis which resulted in the crushing of the Black Douglases has overshadowed by its drama the other events of the reign. The other side of the story of James II's relations with his nobles is much more prosaic, but also much more important. In 1444–5, during his minority, the earldom of Huntly had been created. After the Douglas murder, in 1452, the crown used its patronage to attract or reward support, and created three further earls and a number of lords of parliament; two of these earldoms were short lived, but the third, the earldom of Erroll, was another creation of major significance. Finally in 1457–8 came four more : the earldoms of Argyll, Morton, Rothes and Marischal. The reign of James II in fact saw the first group of creations which brought to the top families who dominated Scottish politics in the sixteenth century; the second group came with James IV. What had happened was that the peerage had been changed beyond recognition; the old Stewart dominance had gone, and the crown now gave influence and high position to families who had served it well, and who were to continue to do so with a remarkable degree of consistency. The Gordons, earls of Huntly, and the Campbells, earls of Argyll, for example, both had a record of crown service which was interrupted in the first case only in the late sixteenth century, and in the second not until the seventeenth, apart from a temporary break in the pattern, for reasons which were understandable, in 1488. Their position as the representatives of royal authority in the north and the west is better known in the sixteenth century, but both James II and James III used them in this role; and if it was a gamble to give men power in fifteenth century Scotland, then the gamble paid off handsomely, for these magnates, while naturally intent on building up their own prestige and dominance, at the same time served the crown both in the central government and in the localities. A striking example of this is seen in the reign of James IV, when the king first instructed the earl of Huntly to take bonds of allegiance to the earl from all the landowners north of the Mounth as a means of giving him formal control; then ordered him to build a tower at Inverlochy as a focal point for royal authority, as exercised by the earl; and finally forgave him for failing to complete it, because his presence had been required at court. This was the busy – and typical – life of a Scottish magnate.

The magnate problem of the early fifteenth century was one of two families, Stewart and Douglas, who had built up too great a concentration of power and wealth. Greed and fear of this power on the part of two strong and ruthless kings had brought them down. After 1455, the issue changes completely. The last years of James II's reign were years of good relations between the crown and all its magnates; years when the power of the crown was seen at its height, when the king, far from feeling that he was the insecure head of a state which was backward by European standards and wracked by an internal power struggle, pursued active and effective policies both abroad and at home. His foreign policy was aggressive and high-handed to the point of making the amazingly arrogant offer of arbitrating in a dispute between the French king and the Dauphin. At home, he showed the same interest in justice as had his father; and so successful was he that in 1458 the parliament which, as it happened, was his last, paid him a fitting and impressive tribute :

God of his grace has send our soverane lorde sik progress and prosperite that all his rebellys and brekaris of his justice ar removit out of his realme, and na maisterfull party remanande that may caus ony breking in his realme;

a comment which incidentally suggests that the king and his most powerful subjects were at one in disliking the potential threat of one family who had too much power and who therefore 'may caus ony breking'.

This period anticipates the reign of James IV, which has always been regarded as one in which the power struggle had abated. It was interrupted by James II's death in 1460, and the problem of another minority, in which the Boyds of Kilmarnock seized temporary control. More serious, however – for the new king had no difficulty in taking over government and bringing down this family in 1468–9 – was the personality of James III himself. In this reign, the problem was not that of the crown taming the magnates; it was the magnates who were trying to tame the crown. The traditional account of James III's downfall, brought about by widespread resentment by the nobles of the king's reliance on lowborn favourites, is legend. James, like many other kings, did have favourites, but they were neither numerous nor lowborn; and the explanation of his failure lies elsewhere. James was a man of grandiose and exalted ideas of kingship, and at the same time a man who was lazy in the business of government and who acted on arbitrary whim. He indulged in wild schemes of continental expansionist campaigns to the extent of giving the impression that all he wanted was to get out of Scotland. He completely failed to understand how to use and gain the trust of his most powerful servants, failing to reward Huntly, for example, for his service against the lord of the Isles in 1476, and giving and taking away lands and offices without reason or justification, thus producing a state of tension and uncertainty among the nobles which prevented any hope of co-operation and good relations. He tried to centralise government in Edinburgh, rarely moving from the capital except on hunting holidays to Falkland. This was an age when Scottish kings were expected to travel throughout their kingdom, being seen by their subjects and taking a personal part in the exercise of justice and the control of the troubled areas of the country, and James' failure to do this increased the idea that this king was remote, uninterested and ineffective. Time and again parliament begged him to do his job properly, pointing out, for example, in 1473 that the business of a king was to govern his country and not to rush off on foreign expeditions. Here it would appear that the magnates were more politically responsible than the crown.

Yet for all this, respect for the monarchy outweighed, for the great majority of the magnates, the fact that James III was personally disastrous. In June 1488, the rebel army at Sauchieburn contained only two earls, Angus, a chronic and individualistic trouble-maker, and Argyll, who had been arbitrarily removed, in February 1488, from the chancellorship which he had held since 1483; and there was also a small number of lords who had suffered from James' high-handed and whimsical actions. Some of the nobility who had given the king active support up to the point where he broke the agreements made with his opponents in April and May, at Aberdeen and Blackness, did not turn up to fight for him at Sauchieburn; possibly after this double-dealing they preferred to solve the problem of the conflict between loyalty to the crown and the feeling that James had finally shown himself impossible to serve by remaining neutral. Others – the majority – continued to support the crown.

1 Caerlaverock Castle, Dumfriesshire

2a Bute or Bannatyne Mazer

2b Detail of the Bute Mazer

3 Lochindorb Castle, Morayshire

4 Elgin Cathedral, Morayshire

5 Tomb of the Wolf of Badenoch in Dunkeld Cathedral

6 Threave Castle, Kirkcudbrightshire

7 Sir Bernard Stewart –
Lord d'Aubigny

8 James III – early portrait coin

9 Angel figures playing musical
instruments, Rosslyn Chapel,
Midlothian

10 James IV (Mytens copy of a contemporary portrait)

11 Andrew Myllar's printing device   12 North West Tower, Holyrood Palace

13 The Great Michael

14 Contemporary drawing of Flodden from *The Trewe Encountre*

15 James V and Mary of Guise

16 Chapel Royal in Falkland Palace, Fife

17 The second Earl of Arran

18 The Fetternear Banner

The rebels of 1488 – surprisingly – won because James was killed, though it is by no means certain that they had wanted a solution as extreme as this. Whatever their aims, however, the nobles who in the reign of James III apparently fitted into the concept of 'overmighty magnates', now became, after 1488, the co-operative nobility of James IV; the same people, not a new and better generation. Angus continued to cause trouble; Huntly, Argyll and others like them to serve the crown. The fifteenth century had been a time of intermittent conflict : James I and the Stewarts, James II and the Douglases, a minority group of the harassed nobility against James III. None of this adds up to a power struggle between 'crown and nobility', with an underlying ideology which caused the crown to regard the magnates as a social and political class as a threat. The situation was very different. King and nobles were recognised, and regarded themselves as the highest ranks in a hierarchical society, a society in which the king, the motivating force in government, relied primarily on the greatest men in his kingdom for counsel and advice and for co-operation in the practical business of running his country. These were the men close to the king; many were his friends, the men who shared his interests and pursuits. In parliament and on the council, while few of them were interested in the minutiae of government, who better to fulfil the traditional role of the king's principal councillors than the magnates, those nearest to him in rank and outlook? And in the localities, who better – indeed, who other – to maintain royal authority than the nobles with their pre-eminent position based on their widespread alliances with their kindreds, the lairds and their tenants and servants, alliances based on protection by the magnates in return for the service and loyalty of their dependants. Fifteenth century Scotland was a unified nation. It was also a network of local societies – and for many, the locality was still more meaningful than the country – in which chances of survival, of safety of life, land and goods, depended on the fulfilling of the contract by which lesser men gave service to the great in return for the very real benefit of their protection and maintenance.

In any case, life for the magnates of fifteenth century Scotland was not always a matter of high politics and feuding. Their interests lay not in opposition to the crown, but in enriching themselves by extending their lands, and the best way to do this was through crown service or by advantageous marriage. They were intensely conscious not simply of their position in the political state, but also of their place in society. To some extent they may have been threatened, as were the nobility in other European countries, by economic pressures; the great were no longer so distinguished by wealth from lesser men as they had formerly been. And the very fact that many of them had been raised from laird to earl or lord also produced pressure to ensure recognition of rank from those who had formerly been their social equals. Thus, for example, the written bond of manrent and service, given by lairds to earls and lords, became a commonplace document in Scotland from the mid-fifteenth century; here was a means of securing formal recognition. And in this century and the next, the government gave its blessing to the increased awareness of social status and desire to define that status in repeated legislation on the dress, the food, the size of retinue which only the great could enjoy; the lesser one's rank, the less elaborate one's style of life. Their self-consciousness in this, their desire to make a splash, is exemplified by the magnificence of the retinue of William, earl of Douglas on his visit to Rome in 1450; the impression this made on the pope was not apparently tinged by any cynicism about the provincial come to town. And if they could not emulate the crown in its acquisition of artillery, that most expensive and supreme status symbol whatever its defects as an effective weapon, they could and did emulate it on a smaller scale in both secular and ecclesiastical building, of which William Sinclair's collegiate church at Roslin is the most striking example. And both Sinclair and Archibald Douglas, earl of Moray, were literary patrons. Some of them sought fortune abroad. This was an obvious outlet for younger sons, many of whom found a profitable career fighting in France, where their value can be seen in the formation by the French monarchy of a Scots Guard in 1445, and where at least one 'soldier of fortune', Bernard Stewart lord d'Aubigny, gained an international reputation. But it was not only younger sons; the earls of Douglas and Buchan both fought in France and were rewarded with French titles before being killed at Verneuil.

The fifteenth century was a time of political upheaval, of redistribution of power and wealth from the hands of two families to a wider, non-royal group. But it was not a time when existing concepts of society, of the place of the crown and the place of the magnates and their close and co-operative relationship to one another was in any way challenged. The early sixteenth century *Porteous of Nobenes,* a work which described the twelve virtues of a nobleman, put second on the list loyalty; the nobles :

ar nocht sa hie set nor ordanit for to reif or tak be force in ony way bot thai ar haldin in werray richt and resoun for to serf thair king and defend there subjectis.

This was not mere literary piety. Many nobles of the fifteenth century did indeed 'serf thair king and defend there subjectis'. At no time did they regard themselves as involved in a power struggle with the monarchy; nor did the crown, which smashed them when they became too powerful, as two families did, and built them up and rewarded them when they served their king. Two magnate families and one king threatened the ideal. But for the rest, they saw themselves, on the whole, as allies.

CHAPTER IV

National Spirit and Native Culture

John MacQueen

Scottish literature, the arts and scholarship in general are often thought to have reached their peak at the court of James IV. The protean character of the king himself – linguist, lover, doctor, builder, alchemist, crusader and rash commander of forlorn hopes – has strengthened the impression that he presided over a great Renaissance court. No fair-minded historian can belittle the accomplishment of the reign, but it must always be made clear that James's reputation has been gained, partly at the expense of his father, James III, partly at that of his son, James V. It is virtually certain, for instance, that the greatest Scottish poet, Robert Henryson, wrote his most important works, the *Testament of Cresseid* and the *Morall Fabillis*, during the reign of James III. Henryson was not, it is true, a court poet in quite the same restricted sense as Dunbar and Lindsay, but he was very much in touch with the major issues of his day, and several of his poems (the *Testament* and *Orpheus and Eurydice* in particular) must have been written with a court audience in mind. Henryson too was essentially a man of the early Northern Renaissance – a Christian humanist, widely interested in the classical inheritance. It is not difficult to see in the *Fabillis* 'the combination of levity with seriousness', which has been described as the common humanistic characteristic of Erasmus and Thomas More. The social satire of the *Fabillis* comes close to that of Book I of More's *Utopia*; indeed one almost establishes that Henryson belonged to the company of the humanists by saying that the social condition of Scotland is one of the main concerns of the *Fabillis*. Henryson pretty certainly was a graduate both in Arts and Law; a marked concern with legal matters is evident both in the *Testament* and in the *Fabillis*. He probably lectured in law at Glasgow University, where he was incorporated in 1462, although it is with Dunfermline that he is chiefly associated as schoolmaster (that is, headmaster) of the ancient grammar school attached to the Benedictine monastery of the town. One may conjecture that he found the humanistic studies of the grammar school more congenial than the often sordid realities of legal pursuits. His poems are based on experience in terms of a wide reading in Latin, French, Scots and English. One may perhaps single out for special mention the use he made of Boccaccio's *Concerning the Genealogy of the Gods,* the universal handbook of the humanist in Italy and elsewhere; a book too which was to have an important influence on Scottish poetry, notably that of Douglas and Lindsay, through much of the following century. During the 1480s Henryson obtained books from the press of William Caxton at Westminster. But his humanism is perhaps most immediately apparent in the additions which he made, or seems likely to have made, to the vocabulary of the English language; they include such words as invention (used of literary creation), capacity, generable, participant, idol, degenerate, rusticate, brutal, diminute, figural, spoliate, irrational, type, toxicate, intricate and vilipend.

It is in fact during the reign of James III that the existence of a literary and artistic Scottish Renaissance begins to be self-evident. The character of the king is difficult to assess, but it is clear that, partly because of his aesthetic and scholarly interests, he was out of sympathy with the general run of the nobility, and much more to the liking of some at least of the artists, craftsmen and writers among his subjects. The most celebrated of his so-called favourites, eventually hanged at Lauder Bridge by the outraged nobility, was Robert Cochrane, the architect of the Great Hall at Stirling Castle, one of the earliest buildings in Great Britain to which the adjective 'Renaissance' may with some fitness by applied. In the full tradition of European royalty, James was himself a collector of fine classical manuscripts. In this, as in other respects, he probably owed a great deal to his former tutor, Archibald Whitelaw, archdeacon of Lothian and sub-dean of Glasgow, who held the office of royal Secretary for the greater part of the reign. Whitelaw was a university man, who had graduated in Arts from St Andrews in 1439, and taught at St Andrews and Cologne before he entered the king's service. The Secretary's office was probably already to some extent a centre of humanistic influence; in James II's reign it had been occupied by William Turnbull, who afterwards, as bishop of Glasgow, became the founder of Glasgow University, and who had also been one of Whitelaw's predecessors as archdeacon of Lothian. Whitelaw belonged to, and expanded, the tradition of Turnbull. Several classical works from his personal library have survived; they include a Lucan, printed at Venice in 1478; a Sallust, printed at Venice in 1481, and Asconius's *Commentaries* on the speeches of Cicero, printed at Venice in 1477. As Secretary, Whitelaw composed a Latin oration, delivered in 1484 at Nottingham to Richard III, which seems to be the earliest extant piece of extended humanistic prose composed by a Scot. It is carefully modelled on Cicero, and in one or two places there are hints that Whitelaw had at least a minimum acquaintance with Greek. Whitelaw survived James III to die in 1498.

Among civil servants and court officials, this humanistic interest continued throughout James IV's reign. The most eminent figure who spans both reigns is William Elphinstone (1431–1514), Keeper of the privy Seal under James IV, bishop of Aberdeen from 1483 onwards, and probably acting archbishop of St Andrews for a brief period after Flodden. Elphinstone was a Glasgow graduate who continued his studies in Paris and lectured at Orleans before his return to Scotland in the early 1470s. His most celebrated achievement was to found the University of Aberdeen in 1495; in addition, he was probably responsible for the Education Act of 1496; for the establishment of Scottish printing in 1507, and for the compilation of the *Breviary of Aberdeen*, printed in two volumes which appeared in 1509 and 1510. The books from his library which survive are mostly legal treatises, but he did possess a manuscript copy of Valla's *Elegantiae*.

Another well-known colleague of Whitelaw was John Reid of Stobo, the 'gud gentill Stobo' of Dunbar's 'Lament for the Makaris', who is thus established as a vernacular poet, once of some reputation. No surviving work, unfortunately, can be attributed to him with any certainty, Stobo however was also described by James III as his 'familiar servant and scribe' when in 1478 he was awarded a pension for life in return for services to the king and his predecessors as a writer of letters to the Pope and diverse kings, princes and magnates outwith the kingdom. In 1497, under James IV, there is record of a payment to Stobo and Walter Chepman 'for thare lawboris in lettrez writing the tyme the King past in Ingland'. (The reference is to the invasion of northern England by James in support of Perkin Warbeck.) It is significant that Stobo's colleague in letter writing was the same Chepman afterwards associated with Andrew Myllar in one of the most notable cultural achievements of James IV's reign, the establishment in 1507 of the first known Scottish printing house. All this at least suggests that Stobo played some part in the fifteenth century movement towards a practical humanism. He died in 1505.

Patrick Paniter (c.1470 – c.1520) became James IV's Secretary in 1507. He was tutor to James's illegitimate and able son, Alexander Stewart, archbishop of St Andrews (1493–1513), who in 1508, perhaps at Paniter's suggestion, became a pupil of Paniter's old contemporary at the College of Montaigu in Paris, the great Erasmus. Stewart and Paniter exchanged a number of affectionate Latin letters. Disappointingly, the surviving volumes of Paniter's library are limited to legal works. Proof of his versatility, and perhaps also of the inefficiency which versatility sometimes entails, is to be found in the fact that he helped to direct the fire of the Scottish artillery at Flodden, the battle in which Stewart, like the king and many others, met his death. Paniter, however, was so fortunate as to escape.

More distinguished still, at least as a writer of humanistic Latin, was Walter Ogilvie, another St Andrews graduate who continued his studies in Paris. Hector Boece, the first Principal of the University of Aberdeen, founded in 1495, and himself a humanist of repute, whose *History of Scotland* was published in 1527, speaks with enthusiasm of the copiousness, the charm and the pithiness of Ogilvie's Latin style. The description may be tested by a long panegyric on Henry VII of England, composed by Ogilvie between 24 January and 2 April 1502, and preserved in the National Library of Scotland in what may be an autograph manuscript. The immediate occasion of the speech is probably the betrothal of Henry VII's daughter Margaret to James IV on 24 January 1502. (The subsequent marriage led, a century later, to the accession of James VI to the throne of England). The panegyric thus offers an interesting Latin parallel to Dunbar's vernacular, *The Thistle and the Rose*. But much of the speech is devoted to Henry's eldest son, Arthur; the latter part consists solely of a description of the ceremonies at the unlucky marriage between Arthur and Catherine of Aragon on 14 November 1501. Ogilvie, it may be, wrote his panegyric because he desired a position at the English court, perhaps as tutor to the young prince, whose death on 2 April 1502, put an end to such ambitions. The panegyric is floridly Ciceronian in style, and answers well enough to Boece's description.

These men, and others like them, were central to the life and activities of James IV's court, and it is no accident that a summary of their careers has involved references to most of the great events of the reign – the foundation of the University of Aberdeen; the Education Act of 1496, which, in theory at least, obliged the eldest sons of barons and freeholders to obtain perfect Latin at grammar school, and then proceed to three years of Arts and Law at University; James's military (and naval) ambitions; the European connections of his court; the Marriage of the Thistle and the Rose; the establishment of printing, and the battle of Flodden. In the same general tradition is the foundation of the Royal College of Surgeons in 1506. The only matter of importance which lies somewhat outside the orbit of the humanists is James's attempt to bring the Highlands, and more particularly the Islands, under direct central administration. The attempt was at least partially successful. In 1493 the semi-independent MacDonald lordship of the Isles came to an end, and in subsequent campaigns James substantially altered the balance of Highland power by establishing the dominance of the Campbells in the west and the Gordons in the north. This process too had a literary monument, the origins at least of which may be traced to James's reign. The oldest considerable body of Scottish Gaelic poetry is preserved in the manuscript *Book of the Dean of Lismore*, compiled between 1512 and 1526 by Sir James MacGregor, Dean of Lismore in Argyll and vicar of Fortingall in Perthshire. The Scottish poems in the collection belong for the most part to the middle and late fifteenth and early sixteenth centuries, and the great majority are court poems, composed not for the royal court (although James did have a command of Gaelic), but for those of the major Highland chiefs, notably the houses owing allegiance to the lords of the Isles, the earls of Argyll, and to the chiefs of clan Gregor. Panegyric, lament and satire are the dominant modes, and there are many references to contemporary events. Here, for instance, is a poem composed by a churchman, the Dean of Knoydart, after the murder (c. 1490) of Angus, son of the Lord of the Isles, by Diarmid Ua Cairbre, an Irish harper:

Thou head of Diarmaid O'Cairbre, though great enough are thy spoils and thy pride, not too great I deem the amount of thy distress though thou hangest from a stake.

I pity not thy shaggy main, nor that it is tossed by the wind of the glens however rough; I pity thee not that a withy is in thy jaws, thou head of Diarmaid O'Cairbre.

Woe to him who hath noted thy throat-stroke, and would not be a foe to thine alliance; woe, alas, to him who rejected not thy shrieks, thou head of Diarmaid O'Cairbre.

By thee was destroyed the king of Islay, a man who dealt wine and silver; whose locks were fresh and crisp, thou head of Diarmaid O'Cairbre.

Islay's king of festive goblets, who raised his friends to honour; woe to him who wounded his bright white skin, thou head of Diarmaid O'Cairbre.

Dear to me was his noble palm, ungrudging of gold or silver; who joyed in feast and hunting, thou head of Diarmaid O'Cairbre.

For Gaelic, the *Book of the Dean* has the same importance as the other great sixteenth century manuscripts – the Asloan, the Bannatyne, the Maitland – have for the vernacular poetry of the Lowlands. Every major aspect of James's reign, and many minor ones, finds expression in this verse, especially in that of the royal court. James, for instance, established a powerful Scottish fleet, the flagship of which was the great *Michael*, the largest warship in Europe, for the construction of which all the woods in Fife are said to have been cut down. A surprising moment in Dunbar's ornate pageant, *The Goldyn Targe*, is the realistic departure of the followers of Venus on board a warship, which fires a salute as they depart:

> In twynkling of ane eye to schip thai went,
> And swyth up saile unto the top thai stent,
> And with swift course atour the flude thay frak;
> Thay fyrit gunnis wyth powder violent,
> Till that the reke raise to the firmament,
> The rochis all resownyt wyth the rak,
> For rede it semyt that the raynbow brak;
> Wyth spirit affrayde apon my fete I sprent
> Amang the clewis, so carefull was the crak.

swyth : *quickly* stent : *stretch* atour : *over* frak : *move swiftly*
rack : *crack* rede : *fear* sprent : *sprang* clewis : *cliffs*

It is fairly obvious that in this poem Dunbar incidentally reflects some of the enthusiasm for naval achievement to be found among his audience at James's court, an enthusiasm fanned by the

E

achievements of commanders like Sir Andrew Wood and the brothers John, Robert and Andrew Barton.

The importance of the burghs steadily increased in the fifteenth and sixteenth centuries. Henryson in the *Taill of the Uponlandis Mous, and the Burges Mous* had already drawn a picture of the slippery prosperity of the rich merchant class. Dunbar continued the tradition, in complimentary terms when he celebrated the welcome given by Aberdeen to the new queen, more critically when he addressed the Merchants of Edinburgh :

> Your proffeit daylie dois incres,
> Your godlie workis les and les;
> Through streittis nane may mak progres
> For cry of cruikit, blind, and lame –

For candid portrayal of the rural life led by the majority, however, it is still better either to turn back to Henryson's *Fabillis*, or forward to Linday with his John the Commonweal and Pauper, the poor man.

Again, the reference to Alexander Stewart has shown that James did not confine his activities to politics, humanism and war. The most celebrated of his mistresses was Lady Margaret Drummond, the eldest daughter of John Drummond, lord of that ilk and of Stobhall in Perthshire. In 1496 she became James's mistress, and in 1502, some nine months before the king's marriage to Margaret Tudor, she and her two sisters were poisoned. Three blue stones mark their grave in the choir of Dunblane Cathedral. James ordered dirges to be sung in Edinburgh, and for years he feed two priests to say masses in the cathedral for the repose of her soul.

The love affair is celebrated in the anonymous *Tayis Bank,* a dream poem, composed perhaps after the lady's death, in which she becomes the central visionary figure in the landscape of the Tay valley :

> To creatur that wes in cair,
> Or cauld of crewelty,
> A blicht blenk of hir vesage bair
> Of baill his bute mycht be.
> Hir hyd, hir hew, hir hevinly hair
> Mycht havy hairtis uphie.
> So angelik under the air
> Never wicht I saw with e.

blicht: *blythe*   blenk: *glance*   bute: *remedy*   hyd: *skin*   uphie: *uplift*

The poem ends with the departure of the lady, and the return of the dreamer to the riverside landscape :

> The rever throw the rise couth rowt,
> And roseris rais on raw.
> The schene birdis full schill couth schowt
> Into that semly schaw.
> Joy wes within and joy without
> Under that wlonkest waw,
> Quhair Tay ran doun with stremis stout
> Full strecht under Stobschaw.

rise : *boughs*   rowt : *roar*   roseris : *rose-bushes* (*'and rose-bushes rose in a row'*)   schene : *bright, beautiful*   schill : *sweet* schaw : *grove*   wlonkest : *fairest*   waw : *wall*

Dunbar in his more direct fashion deals with James and a different mistress in *The Wowing of the King quhen he wes in Dun-fermeling.* The tod (fox) represents the king :

> The tod wes nowder lene nor skowry,
> He wes ane lusty reid haird lowry,
> Ane lang taild beist and grit with all;
> The silly lame wes all to small
> To sic ane tribbill to hald ane bace;
> Scho fled him nocht; fair mot hir fall !
> And that me thocht ane ferly cace.

skowry : *wasted, withered*   lowry : *fox*   tribbill : *treble*   bace : *bass* fair mot hir fall : *good luck to her*   ferly : *wonderful*

Characteristically, even in the marriage pageant of *The Thistle and the Rose*, Dunbar takes James to task on the subject of his mistresses. Dame Nature is addressing the Thistle, king of all plant life, who symbolises certain aspects of the Scottish crown, and thus of the king :

> And sen thow art a king, thow be discreit;
> Herb without vertew thow hald nocht of sic pryce
> As herb of vertew and of odor sueit;
> And lat no nettill vyle, and full of vyce,
> Hir fallow to the gudly flour delyce;
> Nor latt no wyld weid, full of churlichenes,
> Compair hir till the lilleis nobilnes.

Nor half non udir flour in sic denty
As the fresche Ros of cullour reid and quhyt;
For gife thow dois, hurt is thyne honesty,
Conciddering that no flour is so perfyt,
So full of vertew, pleasans, and delyt,
So full of blisfull angeilik bewty,
Imperiall birth, honour and dignite.

pryce : *value*   hir fallow to : *match herself with*   denty : *esteem*

These poems stand well apart from the general achievement of
the humanists. To a considerable extent, however, poets and
humanists belonged to the same company, and emerged from the
same background of university education. Dunbar and Douglas
were both St Andrews graduates, and John Reid of Stobo achieved
distinction both as vernacular poet and as humanist writer of
official Latin epistles. The stylistic brilliance of the makars cor-
responds to the Ciceronian eloquence of the humanists, and mirrors
the same careful training in rhetoric. Stobo, Paniter and Ogilvie
have a natural place among the honourable servants of the king,
as described by Dunbar in *Remonstrance to the King* :

Schir, ye have mony servitouris
And officiaris of dyvers curis;
Kirkmen, courtmen, and craftismen fyne;
Doctouris in jure, and medicyne;
Divinouris, rethoris, and philosophouris,
Astrologis, artistis, and oratouris –

curis : *callings, occupations*   jure : *law, jurisprudence*

Correspondingly, for himself Dunbar makes the classical claim of
immortality through his verse, and it is notable that when Gavin
Douglas in *The Palice of Honour* (1501) lists the eternally famous
poets, he includes not merely such names as Homer, Virgil, Ovid,
Petrarch and Chaucer, but also, to represent Scotland,

Greit Kennedie and Dunbar yit undeid
And Quintine with ane Huttok on his heid.

Huttok : *some kind of hat*

Even in his lifetime, that is to say, Dunbar was regarded by his
contemporaries as a classic. It is worth noting too that by implica-
tion Douglas places himself in the same high company.

Douglas in fact, by his life as by his poetry, stands most obviously in the tradition of the court humanists. *The Palice of Honour* with its emphasis on the nine classical Muses, and a concept of Honour which is subsumed finally in the person of the God of *Revelation*, is essentially a manifesto of the movement. Douglas included among the scholars and poets admitted to the palace the founders of the Italian Renaissance, Petrarch, Boccaccio, Poggio, Valla and Pomponius Laetus. He refers to Valla and Boccaccio in the prologue to the first book of his translation of Virgil's *Aeneid*, completed in 1513, the year of Flodden. In the prologue to the sixth book he mentions the Dutch humanist, Jodocus Badius Ascensius, whose commentary he used extensively. But of course the mere existence of Douglas's *Aeneid*, the first and best of the great Renaissance translations of the British Isles, is the clearest proof of the European accomplishment and classical scholarship of James's court :

> The batalis and the man I wil discrive
> Fra Troyis boundis first that fugitive
> By fait to Ytail come and cost Lavyne,
> Our land and sey katchit with mekil pyne
> By fors of goddis abufe, from euery steid,
> Of cruell Iuno throu ald remembrit fede.
> Gret pane in batail sufferit he alsso
> Or his goddis brocht in Latio
> And belt the cite fra quham, of nobill fame,
> The Latyne pepill takyn heth thar name,
> And eik the faderis, princis of Alba,
> Cam, and the wallaris of gret Rome alswa.

discrive : *describe, record*   katchit : *driven, tossed*   mekil : *great*
pyne : *distress, suffering*   steid : *place*   fede : *enmity, hatred*
or : *before*   belt : *built*   wallaris : *wall builders*   alswa : *also, as well*

Dunbar and Douglas are the greatest individual poets of James's reign. In many ways, however, a lesser figure – John Major (1470–1550), theologian and historian, student of Cambridge and Paris, professor at Paris, Glasgow and St Andrews, commonly called 'the last of the schoolmen' – is more respresentative of the general style of the era. It may seem almost paradoxical to include such a man in an account, the primary emphasis of which lies on the Renaissance. In fact the paradox is more apparent than real. Admittedly, Major's immediate intellectual concerns were those which had occupied the theologians of the twelfth, thirteenth and fourteenth centuries; his way of thought and expression lies deliberately close to theirs. In this, however, he differs scarcely at all from the majority of his immediate contemporaries – from Dunbar, for instance, at least under the aspect of priest and writer of magnificent vernacular hymns in the full medieval tradition :

> Syng hevin imperiall, most of hicht,
> Regions of air make armony;
> All fishe in flud and foull of flicht
> Be myrthfull and mak melody :
> All *Gloria in excelsis* cry,
> Hevin, erd, se, man, bird, and best,
> He that is crownit abone the sky
> *Pro nobis Puer natus est.*

hevin imperiall : *empyreal heaven, the dweling of God and his angels*

But Major was well aware that the world for which he wrote had changed vastly over the centuries, and the changes have left traces in his works. For instance, in the dedication of the *Quartus Sententiarum* to Alexander Stewart, he defends the theological Latin which Stewart, as we have seen, had been trained to regard as barbarous. And of course the mere fact that Major, a theologian, wrote history, is significant – in the context of his times one might almost say revolutionary. The logical methods which he used sometimes led to important advances. One may illustrate by a story which links Major with his friend Gavin Douglas, and which is preserved by the Italian historian and humanist, Polydore Vergil, who sought information on the early Scottish kings from Douglas, while the latter was in London during the last months of his life.

Of late one Gawine Dowglas, Bishop of Dunchell, a Scottishe man, a manne as well noble in ligniage as vertewe, when he understoode that I was purposed to write this historie, hee camme to commune with me; in forthe with, we fell into friendshippe, and after he vehementlie requiered mee, that in relation of the Scottishe affaires, I showlde in no wise follow the president of an historie of a certaine contriman of his . . .

The countryman was Major who in his *History* (1521) had dismissed much of the traditional history of Scotland as fable. Douglas provided Polydore as an alternative with the usual story of Gathelus and Scota, daughter of Pharaoh. Polydore was not convinced.

As soon as I hadde redde these thinges, accordinge to the olde proverbe, I seemed to see the beare bringe foorthe her younglinges. ... Wherefore I towlde him, even as frindlie as trewlie, that as concerninge the Scottes and Pictes beefore there comminge into Brittaine (which Bedas in his time hadd well assigned), it showlde not bee lawful for me to intermeddell, bie reason of the prescript which is incident to an historien, which is that hee showld nether abhorre the discooveringe of falsehoode, nether in anie case alowe the undermininge of veritee, nether to gyve suspition of favor nor yeat of envy. This Gawine, noe doubte a sincere manne, didd the lesse dissent from this sentence, in that it plainlie appeared to him that reason and trewthe herin well agreaed, so easilie is trewthe allwaise discovowred from feyned phansies.

Schoolman and man of all the full Renaissance are here momentarily at one (Polydore, however, carried his doubts further than Major), and Douglas at least begins by adhering to older superstitions – although it is notable that he was open to rational conviction by Polydore. Major too is well aware that the style and method of his history is unusual, but he is prepared to defend himself. For him, as for the earlier Whitelaw and Ogilvie, the most distinguished historians are the humanist idols, Sallust and Livy – interestingly he adds Bede to the company – but he pleads the passage of time, that sixteenth century Scotland differs significantly from pagan Rome. He adds that theology is a training peculiarly appropriate for the writer of history, who must make distinctions. 'And, indeed, I have given my utmost endeavour to follow this course in all cases, and most of all where the question was ambiguous, to the end that from the reading of this history you may learn not only the thing that was done, but also how it ought to have been done, and that you may by this means and at the cost of little reading come to know what the experience of centuries, if it were granted to you to live so long, could scarcely teach.' Such an idea of history reaches back beyond Sallust or Livy to the greatest Greek historian, Thucydides.

Major thus provides much interesting material on the intellectual climate in which he lived, and it is all the more interesting because he himself appears to have been singularly broadminded and tolerant in his treatment of ideas and the effects which they had on his contemporaries. Thus he is an advocate of political union between Scotland and England. He nowhere directly attacks the views of Erasmus, who had been a student in the same college as himself in Paris. He is acquainted with the Latin works of Petrarch and Pico della Mirandola. He was clearly aware that Gavin Douglas, then Provost of St Giles in Edinburgh, held views on theological method very different from his own, but he made no direct attack on Douglas; instead he prefixed to his *In primum Sententiarum* a Latin *Dialogue concerning the material appropriate to the Theologian*, in which the speakers are Gavin Douglas himself, and David Cranston, one of the most distinguished of Major's pupils, who like Major himself had some knowledge of Greek. Douglas is given a full and friendly opportunity to state his views, which are very much those of the Renaissance. Theologians are too much concerned with Aristotelian subtleties, not enough with the fathers of the church and with Scripture; they write too much and too little to the purpose; they are arrogant. He quotes Laurentius Valla to support his position. Cranston replies that theological methods have more value for some than for others; that Major himself has always been opposed to needless verbosity, and that Douglas is attacking, not theological method itself, but the inappropriate use of theological method. He dismisses the views of Valla as those of a lunatic; Valla made more mistakes in his dialectic than there are spots on a leopard. Douglas parts amicably from Cranston reminding him that Major's birthplace at Gleghornie is only 'a sabbath journey in the law of Moses' from his own at Tantallon. Douglas and Major, incidentally, held identical opinions on at least one matter, the scholarly achievement of the first English printer, William Caxton. Douglas justifiably has no good word for Caxton's *Aeneid*; rather less justifiably Major despises Caxton's edition of Trevisa's translation of the historian Higden's *Polychronicon*, which he probably believed was the printer's own composition. But at least Major made some attempt to be judicious, even about Caxton. 'Now in a measure, if not altogether,' he says, 'we may make allowance for an unlettered man : he followed simply the fashion of speech that was common amongst the English about their enemies, the Scots.'

In conclusion, two points must be emphasised. In James's reign, the Scottish Reformation was still a matter of the far future. At the same time, many of the characteristics of the reformers were already visible in isolation among individuals, and the society in which these individuals lived was particularly open to reformation influences. Dunbar combines an intense imaginative experience of catholicism with disillusion about the state of the society and the position of the church within that society :

> Kirkmen so halie ar and gude,
> That on thair conscience, rowme and rude,
> May turn aucht oxin and ane wane.

rowme : *broad* rude : *rough* aucht : *eight* wane : *wagon, cart (the eight ox team was the usual haulage unit)*

or :

> Quhat help is thair in lordschips sevin,
> Quhone na hous is bot hell and hevin,
> Palice of lycht, or pit obscure?

The extraordinary appointment of a gifted boy, a royal bastard, to the primatial see of St Andrews cannot have strengthened the church, any more than did the excommunication of James at the end of his reign by Pope Julius and his successor Pope Leo, whose main intention was to keep France in political isolation, and who found an excuse, when James, in violation of the treaty of peace which he had signed in 1502, at last invaded England. The abstract and courteous debate between Major and Douglas held the potential of the very different style later adopted by John Knox and George Buchanan.

Secondly, the idea that Flodden was the crowning disaster of Scottish history, and that the achievements of national spirit and native culture which had preceded it came to an end with the death of James IV will not bear close examination. The supreme tragedy of Flodden is a romantic myth. The careers of several of the men discussed in this chapter continued as if the battle had never taken place. Culturally, the achievement of James V's reign compares very favourably with what had gone before. In literature, in architecture and in music, pre-Reformation Scotland still had much to accomplish when the infant James V succeeded his brilliant father.

CHAPTER V

Flodden and its Aftermath

Caroline Bingham

'Inevitable' is a word too much beloved of historians; the appearance of inevitability derives most often from the advantage of hindsight. Yet this said, there is an appearance at least of inexorability in the chain of events which led from the marriage of James IV and Margaret Tudor in 1503 to the fatal battlefield of Flodden in 1513.

The marriage had been discussed as early as 1495, when Margaret was aged about seven. The marriage negotiations, however, were preceded by negotiations for a treaty of perpetual peace between Scotland and England. The treaty, concluded in 1502, was made under papal confirmation, with automatic excommunication laid upon which ever party should break the peace. The marriage took place in August of the following year.

James IV, desirous of maintaining peace on all fronts, and at the same time of safeguarding himself against political domination by England, declined specifically to repudiate Scotland's traditional alliance with France. Peace with both England and France remained feasible as long as Henry VII reigned. The delicacy of James's position was revealed soon after Henry VIII succeeded in 1509.

Henry VII had been too concerned in consolidating his hold upon the English throne to indulge in military adventures abroad, besides which he had been restrained by his essential parsimony from indulging in the vast expense of warfare. Neither consideration applied with Henry VIII. He was young and hot-headed, and ambitious for military glory, which he hoped to gain by recovering some of England's lost territories in France, emulating Henry V.

The involvement of France in the Italian Wars provided his opportunity. In 1511 Pope Julius II formed his mis-named 'Holy League' to expel the French from Italy, and the following year Henry allied himself with the Papacy, Spain, Venice and the Emperor Maximilian, and prepared to invade France in the name of the Holy League. In 1513 his invasion culminated in a pointless but satisfyingly 'glorious' victory at Guinegate.

James IV had watched these events with mounting anxiety. Henry VIII, from the beginning of his reign, had shown a high-handed and bellicose attitude towards Scotland, and James had soon begun to doubt the permanency of the perpetual peace. In 1512, at the urgent request of Louis XII of France, James agreed to a formal renewal of the auld alliance. He was thus in the unhappy position of being committed to both France and England when Henry VIII invaded France.

James IV has often been condemned as quixotically chivalrous for launching a counter-invasion in response to the pleas of his French ally; but in fact the deterioration of relations between Scotland and England left him little choice but to revert to the traditional policy of the auld alliance. On 22 August 1513 he invaded England and proceeded to reduce three fortresses, Norham, Etal and Ford, which served the double purpose of safeguarding his line of retreat, and drawing northward the English army, commanded by the earl of Surrey. The two armies met near Flodden Edge in Northumberland where, on 9 September, James IV was defeated and slain.

It was said by a contemporary that James's principal fault as a general was that 'he begins to fight even before he has given his orders'. No doubt it was his primitive heroism that cost him his life, but what in fact cost the Scots the battle was the effectiveness of the English artillery and the technological superiority of the English in other weapons. The Scots were armed with fifteen-foot wooden spears, the English with bills, which had an eight-foot shaft and a long, axe-like blade terminating in a spike. The Scottish spearmen, with the king, charged downhill, irresistible as long as they kept moving. When their impetus was halted, in muddy ground at the foot of Flodden Edge, they found their long weapons useless against the bills of the English. The shafts of their spears were sliced through by the blades of the bills, and spearmen who managed to draw their swords were still defenceless against the longer reach of their adversaries. It was in this *mêlée* that the king died, not at the last, surrounded by a 'dark, impenetrable wood' of spears.

Traditionally, Flodden has always been regarded as one of the great disasters of Scottish history, and small wonder since the king himself died, and with him the archbishop of St Andrews (the king's illegitimate son), two other bishops, three abbots, one dean, fourteen earls, about the same number of lords, three Highland chiefs, and a great number of lairds, variously estimated. However, recent research has tended to reduce earlier estimates of the number of the nameless dead, especially among the Borderers, those very 'Flowers of the Forest' whom the romanticism of later generations particularly lamented. And, as Professor Donaldson has rightly remarked, there was 'nothing novel about a heavy defeat at the hands of the English, and Flodden was neither the first nor the last in a long series'.

Flodden was a disaster principally in that it occasioned the loss of a king who was the guiding spirit of the nation. It brought to an end an epoch of growing prosperity and creativity which might have continued and developed even more remarkably had James IV lived longer.

In historical perspective, however, the significance of Flodden was not merely that of a massive defeat which caused the loss of an able king and the end of a period of stability, its significance was rather that of an event which reshaped Scotland's future through the changing political attitudes which resulted from it. The history of the aftermath of Flodden is the history of Scotland's growing disillusionment with the auld alliance, and in consequence of that disillusionment, the painfully reluctant drawing together of Scotland and England, especially under the influence of developing protestantism.

Immediately after Flodden the seventeen-month-old James V was crowned king, and in accordance with the will of James IV Margaret Tudor was appointed tutrix or guardian of her son, which made her in effect the head of state, although she did not enjoy the title of regent.

Her position as head of state was not in itself acceptable to the most powerful of the men associated with her in the government. James Hamilton, 1st earl of Arran, James Beaton, archbishop of Glasgow, and Alexander 3rd Lord Home, the High Chamberlain, opposed Margaret largely because she was the sister of the king who had not only inflicted upon Scotland a disastrous defeat, but had also made clear his basic attitude towards Scotland to the herald of James IV who visited him in France immediately before the Flodden campaign. 'I am the very owner of Scotland,' Henry had said, 'and he (James IV) holdeth it of me by homage.' This clear statement of Henry's renewal of the medieval English kings' claim to overlordship of Scotland naturally made the more nationally-conscious members of the Scottish government unwilling to accept a Tudor as head of state.

The most obvious alternative to Margaret, and the most acceptable candidate in accordance with Scottish theory, was the heir presumptive, John, duke of Albany. He was the son of James III's treacherous brother, Alexander, duke of Albany, by his French wife, Agnès de la Tour d'Auvergne. Born and brought up in France, the country to which Alexander had been banished, John, duke of Albany was a veritable personification of the auld alliance.

Margaret played into the hands of the pro-Albany party by her marriage to Archibald Douglas, 6th earl of Angus, in 1514 since under the terms of James IV's will she was to be tutrix of the king only so long as she should remain a widow. Upon her re-marriage she was forced to resign her position and consent to the appointment of Albany as regent.

Albany, who spent three periods of residence in Scotland between 1515 and 1524, was an able and conscientious man who attempted to balance the duty which he felt towards the French King Francis I with the duty which he owed as regent to James V. This proved a thankless task since the Scots felt keenly that at Flodden they had fought and sustained a heavy defeat on behalf of an ungrateful ally. Indeed, the appointment of Albany as regent was very much more a device to exclude Margaret Tudor than a pro-French appointment. This was made clear by two recurrences of enmity with England in 1522 and 1523, both consequent upon hostilities between Francis I and Henry VIII. On both occasions Albany attempted to lead a Scottish army into England, on the latter occasion an army reinforced with French troops and artillery. But on both occasions the army advanced as far as the Border, only to refuse actual invasion. These two manifestations of the so-called 'Flodden complex' did not illustrate that the Scots shrank from facing the English in the field, but that they were unwilling to sustain further loss on behalf of France. They were firm in insisting that defence and not attack was all that could be asked of them.

When Albany left Scotland in the spring of 1524, his influence weakened by two inglorious and unpopular military expeditions, his political opponents had an opportunity to seize power and reverse his policy. The Scots did not appreciate that Albany's regency had probably saved the country from English domination. They were aware only that Francis I had attempted to manipulate Scotland in his own interests, and that the auld alliance had been too frequently invoked to make Scotland the tool of French policy. However, the alternative was that Henry VIII would attempt to make Scotland an English satellite through the influence of Margaret and her husband Angus.

Had there been any reasonable degree of concord between Margaret and Angus, it is possible that Henry could have developed a strong enough pro-English party to have achieved his objective. But between them there was not only marital disharmony but conflicting ambition. Margaret, usually a staunch supporter of her brother, was temporarily estranged from him when he refused to assist her in obtaining a divorce from Angus; indeed, it was by cultivating Albany, who was related by marriage to the Medici, the family of Pope Clement VII, that she finally gained her divorce. After that it was remarked that Henry 'never carried such respect to his sister as he had done before'.

In 1524, after Albany's departure, Margaret briefly regained control of the king, and supported by Arran, her position as head of state. But a year later Angus secured the person of the king by a coup d'état. James V remained a virtual prisoner of the Douglas faction, which enjoyed the support of Henry VIII, until 1528.

James therefore spent some of his most influential formative years in the hands of the Douglases. His education had been abandoned before he was thirteen, leaving him with a somewhat inadequate grounding in French and Latin, a poor standard of education by comparison with that of most Renaissance princes. By the time he was fifteen or so the Douglases, according to George Buchanan, with a cynical disregard for the king's welfare 'made him more inclinable to women, because by that means they hoped to have him longer under their tuition'. However, a course of systematic spoiling and incitement to immorality did nothing to blunt the king's intelligence. During his unwilling sojourn with the Douglases James developed into a shrewd and observant young man, with strong ideas of his own, which he was capable of keeping to himself until he was free to act upon them. He became, therefore, mentally somewhat isolated and, again according to Buchanan, 'naturally suspicious'.

James had learnt from his mother to dislike and distrust Angus. His own experience at Angus's hands turned those feelings into a lasting detestation which he extended from Angus himself to almost every other member of the house of Douglas. Furthermore, since Angus was the principal agent of English influence in Scotland, the English alliance became repugnant to James V, together with the faction which supported it.

In 1528, at the age of sixteen, James escaped from the Douglases, and within a few months was able to assert his authority and banish his former gaolers. Angus and his principal kinsmen, forfeited and under sentence of death, fled the country and placed themselves in the protection of Henry VIII.

In the interstices of Albany's regency and following his departure the strife of factions in Scotland had been largely a matter of family ambition. Arran and his Hamilton kindred and been pro-French in that they opposed the Douglases. But both groups were principally concerned to use the influence of foreign powers for their own aggrandizement. The Douglases were always for the Douglases; the Hamiltons were interested basically in their reversionary rights to the Scottish throne. With the emergence of the king, factionary attitudes were submerged in a national policy once more.

James V, concerned to maintain his freedom of action against England, was obliged to turn to the auld alliance. As an eighteenth century historian expressed it, Henry 'in supporting the infamous Douglases against their sovereign . . . in a manner forced James to fix a connexion with France'. But there were certain advantages to be looked for from France : for instance, the Treaty of Rouen, negotiated by Albany in 1517 and ratified in 1521, promised James marriage with a daughter of Francis I, and a mutual offensive and defensive alliance against England.

Francis I, whose policy throughout his reign was shaped by his rivalry with the Emperor Charles V, long remained reluctant to take up a definitely anti-English standpoint by honouring the Treaty of Rouen. James V, however, responded with patience and astuteness. Though eager to bring Francis to a decision – not only for political but for financial reasons, since he stood in great need of a French princess's dowry – James played skilfully upon Francis' basic unwillingness to see him marry elsewhere by inviting counter-proposals. After prolonged negotiations with the

Emperor, with the deposed King of Denmark, with the Pope, for the hand of his ward Catherine de Medici, and even with Henry VIII, James at last persuaded Francis I to part with his daughter Madeleine, and a dowry of 100,000 livres. The marriage took place in Paris on 1 January 1537. Madeleine died within the year, but James reaffirmed his fidelity to the auld alliance by marrying a second French bride, Mary of Guise-Lorraine, in 1538.

James was able to follow a pro-French policy as long as it did not involve him in military action on behalf of France; but when enmity with England was renewed at the end of the reign the latent unpopularity of his policy was quickly revealed. And throughout the reign the unpopularity of his foreign policy was enhanced by that of a domestic policy equally ill-calculated to commend itself to the most influential class of his subjects.

The natural result of a minority in which he had been the prisoner of a turbulent subject was that James reached adulthood with a particular determination to impose a strong discipline upon the nobility. At the same time, the authoritarianism of James V should be seen not only in its Scottish but also its European context, for James shared the preoccupations common to Renaissance sovereigns. Like Francis I and Henry VIII, James V was absolutist in his aims, concerned to increase the power of the Crown, to reduce the nobility as far as possible to a condition of dependence, and to develop an administration served by men who were not of noble family and therefore had no inherent belief in their own independence. Much of this remained greatly beyond his scope, but his aims were clear enough.

James's determination to discipline his nobility accompanied a desire to impose law and order throughout his realm. He began with those perennial problem areas, the Borders, the Highlands and the Isles.

His first expedition to the Borders took place in the spring of 1529 and resulted in the execution of two notorious reivers, Scott of Tushielaw and Cockburn of Henderland. The following spring he made his famous raid upon the Armstrongs of Liddesdale, who had boasted that they acknowledged the authority neither of the King of England nor the King of Scots. The result was the execution of Armstrong of Mangerton, the head of the family, and his brother Armstrong of Gilnockie, the 'Johnie Armestrong' of the well-known ballad. As a result of this rough justice, and of spells of imprisonment endured by various Border magnates, including the earl of Bothwell, Lords Home and Maxwell, and the lairds of Johnston, Polwarth, Ferniherst and Buccleuch, the Borders were quietened, and remained so for the rest of the reign.

The western Highlands and the Isles presented a conjoint problem. During the king's minority and under Angus's regime the keeping of order in the whole area had been entrusted to the 3rd earl of Argyll, who died in 1529. James, deeply suspicious of the immense influence wielded by his family, the Campbells, took the opportunity to reduce the official powers of the 4th earl by refusing him the commission of Lieutenancy of the Isles which had been held by his father, and granting it instead to his enemy MacDonald of Islay, who had informed the king that the Campbell policy had been to foment disorder in the Isles and then gain credit and profit by stamping it out. Argyll spent a short spell in prison in 1531, and therafter remained out of favour for several years. The Isles remained quiet until 1539, when a rebellion broke out led by Donald Gorm of Sleat, who laid claim to the lordship of the Isles which had so long maintained an existence almost independent of the Crown of Scots. The rebellion was abortive, but no doubt its occurrence influenced the king in his decision to make a circumnavigation of the north in 1540.

The king's voyage was conceived partly as a royal progress, to illustrate the splendour and authority of the sovereign, and partly as a naval expedition, to overawe unruly and potentially rebellious subjects. Twelve ships, heavily equipped with artillery, carried the king and his entourage from Leith, up the east coast and across the Pentland Firth to Orkney, thence around Cape Wrath to the Isles of Lewis, Harris, North and South Uist and to Skye. James landed also upon Coll, Tiree and Mull, Arran and Bute, and ended his voyage at Dumbarton.

The voyage had taken him to some outlying parts of his kingdom previously unvisited by any kings of his house. It had enabled him to pursue his policy of placing lesser men dependent upon himself in positions customarily occupied by members of the greater nobility, by appointing his favourite Oliver Sinclair as sheriff of Orkney – no bad choice since Oliver Sinclair was a cadet of the family of the earls of Caithness and Orkney, yet nonetheless dependent upon the king for his advancement. More importantly the voyage enabled James to take prisoners and hostages from

F

several clans whose loyalty he doubted. His prisoners included John Mackenzie, chief of the Clan Mackenzie, Hector Maclean of Duart and James Macconel of Islay. He also brought home with him a number of chieftains' sons, for education at court, with the hope, no doubt, of producing a more tractable generation to succeed to estates in a notoriously turbulent part of his kingdom. Finally, the voyage enabled the king to annexe the lordship of the Isles to the Crown. The annexation was enacted by the parliament which met in the winter of 1540, following the king's return. James's companions on his voyage were Oliver Sinclair, the 4th earl of Huntly and Cardinal Beaton.

Huntly, James's cousin and his only friend among the greater nobility, had been responsible for keeping law and order in the north throughout the reign. The power of his family, the Gordons, in the north equalled that of the Campbells in the west; but James made no inroads upon it, and he seems to have been justified in his confidence that Huntly would use his power in the interest of the Crown. Huntly was to emerge as a turbulent subject in the reign of James' daughter.

James's unpopularity with the nobility arose from two causes: the harshness of his disciplinary measures, and the acquisitiveness he showed in attempting to build up the finances of the Crown. From their own viewpoint the nobles had cause for complaint: Angus was in exile throughout the reign, Argyll, Bothwell, Moray, Home and Maxwell were all imprisoned at one time and another; the 8th earl of Crawford was mulcted of large sums of money and his son was compelled to resign his succession to the earldom; the 3rd earl of Morton was forced to resign his lands to his kinsman Douglas of Lochleven, who made them over to the king; and Hamilton of Finnart, the illegitimate son of Arran and at one time a favourite of the king, was suddenly put on trial for treason and executed, according to contemporary opinion chiefly because James coveted his wealth. It was little wonder that, as Norfolk informed Henry VIII, 'so sore a dread king, and so ill-beloved of his subjects was never in that land'.

It must be remarked that James's unpopularity with his nobility contrasted sharply with his popularity with the common people. The king's desire to see law and order imposed throughout the kingdom, and the severity with which he pursued and punished malefactors, made him in the eyes of the defenceless mass of his subjects their champion and protector. In this his popularity was well enough deserved. It was further enhanced by his fondness for slipping away from the ceremonial of his court and wandering about the countryside disguised, perhaps rather ineffectually, as a farmer. The adventures which he encountered in the guise of the 'Gudeman of Ballengeich' belong rather to folklore than to history.

The Gudeman of Ballengeich is a pleasanter aspect of James V than that of the covetous oppressor of the nobility. But perhaps it is a somewhat extenuating circumstance that James's acquisitiveness did not arise from mere avarice. Though it was truly observed that he 'marvellously enriched' himself, he also spent lavishly on patronage of the arts, especially architecture. A lavish building programme, mostly of decorative schemes completing works begun in his father's reign, was undertaken in the later years of James V. The grandest surviving examples of the patronage of James V are at Stirling and Falkland.

When James went to France to marry the Princess Madeleine, he spent some months as the guest of Francis I, at Blois, Chambord and Fontainbleau amongst other places. With the evident wish of making his own royal palaces worthy of comparison with those of France, he set about superimposing upon his still basically medieval residences the appearance of Renaissance châteaux. At Stirling James V's 'Palace' displays a riot of Renaissance sculpture, reminiscent of Blois, which covers a building begun in the reign of James IV. Similarly, the courtyard facade of the south wing at Falkland shows the Renaissance embellishment of a late Gothic structure. At Holyrood James V added an imposing main facade to the existing James IV Tower. But his buildings were damaged in the earl of Hertford's invasion of 1544, and were finally demolished to make way for Charles II's complete scheme of reconstruction. Linlithgow is a palimpsest of all architectual styles from the reign of James III to that of James VI; but the gatehouse complete belongs to that of James V.

Upon these works, and their commensurably rich interiors, of which little survives but the series of oak medallions known as the 'Stirling Heads' now on display at Stirling Castle, James V spent much of the money which his nobles were forced to disgorge. Posterity may be grateful to him, though they were not.

James's unpopularity with the nobility led him to rely disproportionately upon the support of the church. Gavin Dunbar, archbishop of Glasgow, was chancellor from 1528 onwards, and Cardinal Beaton was James's chief adviser from 1538 to the end of the reign. Furthermore, the church provided James with two important sources of finance : commendams and taxation. James V secured the appointment of several of his illegitimate sons as commendators or titular abbots of the richest abbeys in Scotland : Kelso, Melrose, St Andrews, Coldingham, the Abbey of Holyrood and the Charterhouse of Perth. He was able to extract even larger sums in taxation. The most impressive instance was the foundation of the College of Justice in 1532 which provided an excuse for imposing upon the church a tax of £10,000 a year, ostensibly for the payment of judicial salaries, in reality almost exclusively for the benefit of the Crown. Ultimately the Scottish prelates compounded for the sum of £72,000 to be paid in four instalments. Much of the money James gained from the church contributed to his building programme. The Pope sanctioned and the church endured taxation on this scale as the price of James V's refusal to follow Henry VIII's example in repudiating papal supremacy and participating in the Reformation.

James V was a catholic by personal conviction and by policy. He supported the church in attempting to prevent the spread of Reformation ideas in Scotland, and he countenanced a limited amount of persecution to this end. Attempts to stem the spread of the Reformation to Scotland had begun as early as 1525, when an act of parliament forbade the import of Lutheran books. Nonetheless, they continued to arrive, mostly coming in through the east coast ports, especially St Andrews where the university became a nursery of Lutheran ideas. At St Andrews occurred the first protestant martyrdom, that of Patrick Hamilton, who was burnt in 1528. He was the author of a widely read religious treatise; setting forth Lutheran opinions. His fame, together with the fact that he was a relative of the king and a martyr who died with the most exemplary courage, served to spread his opinions with a speed which was intensely alarming to the church. A second martyrdom took place in 1532 or 3 also at St Andrews, and in 1534 the king himself presided at the trial of two men named Straiton and Gourlay, who were duly burnt. In 1532 an act of parliament had recorded his resolution to 'defend the authority, liberty and freedom of the seat of Rome and halikirk'. But from 1534 onwards James came under considerable diplomatic pressure to imitate the religious policy of Henry VIII. It was in the matter of religion that James's domestic and foreign policy interacted, ultimately to his detriment, for his catholicism was integrally related to his determination to maintain alliance with France.

Henry did all he could to prevent the marriage of James and Madeleine, and after Madeleine's death he attempted to prevent James from marrying Mary of Guise by negotiating to marry her himself. Even after James had affirmed his fidelity to the auld alliance by his second French marriage, Henry sent Sir Ralph Sadler to Scotland in 1540, with instructions to attempt to undermine the influence of Cardinal Beaton, and to point out to James the financial advantages of imitating Henry's policy in dissolving religious foundations and annexing church property. James, however, stoutly affirmed his confidence in Cardinal Beaton, and on the subject of the Scottish abbeys pointedly demanded of Sadler 'What need I to take them to increase my livelihood, when I may have anything that I can require of them?'

In their relations with each other James and Henry were principally motivated by fear. James, not without reason, feared Henry's ultimate intention in seeking to extend the Henrician Reformation to Scotland; he feared in the background the old claim to overlordship which Henry had overtly voiced in 1513 and covertly sought to make good during James's own minority. Henry on his side feared the auld alliance, since a rapprochement between Francis I and the Emperor led him to fear the formation of a Franco-Imperial alliance against heretical England; and since the league between France and Scotland had become so close he felt intensely vulnerable to a tripartite league and to the possibility of invasion from the north.

In an atmosphere of mutual fear and mistrust relations between the two sovereigns deteriorated during 1541, and by the following year the outbreak of war seemed unavoidable. In 1542 the triangular relationship of Scotland, England and France was not unlike that of 1513, but the old configuration was altered by a new element – the influence of protestantism. It was as the ally of both France and the Papacy that James V faced enmity with England in the last year of his reign. In addition to the post-Flodden unpopularity of the auld alliance, James had to contend with the unpopularity of his own domestic policy. His dependence upon the church had helped to give his bad relations with the nobility a religious slant. In the course of his reign a large number of his influential subjects had embraced protestantism, and it was widely believed that James kept a blacklist of 350 nobles against whom he could institute proceedings for heresy if he chose, and that the blacklist was headed by the name of James's Hamilton cousin, the 2nd earl of Arran.

With the outbreak of war James's nobility refused to follow him in an invasion of England, and at Solway Moss on 25 November 1542, the Scottish army suffered a disgraceful defeat at the hands of a very much smaller English force. After little resistance the army scattered and many nobles were taken prisoner, seemingly eager to surrender rather than die in the service of an unpopular king and for the sake of an unpopular policy. On 14 December James himself died at Falkland, the victim apparently of a complete mental and physical breakdown. He left as his heir a baby girl, Mary, Queen of Scots, aged one week.

Each year of Mary's minority brought closer the ultimate victory of protestantism in Scotland; yet the succession of events during the minority gave no impression that the victory was inevitable. The auld alliance was closest in the last year of its existence.

On the death of James V Mary of Guise did not become head of state as Margaret Tudor had done in 1513. Possibly Mary was too closely identified with the unpopular policy of James V. After a brief power struggle the regency fell to the man designated by precedent, the heir presumptive, James Hamilton, 2nd earl of Arran. Cardinal Beaton was imprisoned and Mary of Guise temporarily relegated to the position merely of Dowager Queen.

In July 1543 Arran negotiated with Henry VIII the Treaties of Greenwich, a peace treaty between Scotland and England and a treaty of marriage between the infant Queen of Scots and Henry's heir Prince Edward. It was further agreed that the queen should be sent to live at the English court. Arran was rewarded with a promise of the hand of Henry's daughter Elizabeth for his eldest son. Cardinal Beaton, however, secured his freedom in September. He quickly achieved an ascendancy over Arran, and in December caused the Treaties of Greenwich to be repudiated. His action led to the English invasions of 1544 and 1545, in which Henry showed his resentment by a devastation of the Borders and the Lothians which the Scots named the 'Rough Wooing'.

The suffering caused by this devastation aroused a resurgence of anti-English feeling in southern Scotland which was as violent as it was short-lived. Henry VIII died in 1547, and the earl of Hertford, who had led the invasions, became duke of Somerset and regent for Edward VI, He continued Henry's policy by invading Scotland in 1547, when he won the battle of Pinkie, which caused the Scots severe losses but achieved nothing politically. Oddly enough, even at the time of Pinkie the tide of anti-English feeling was receding, for the auld enemy seemed only half so inimical when Scotland and England had come to contain many Protestant co-religionists; and the danger that Scotland would become an English province in the reign of Edward VI was finally frustrated when Mary of Guise arranged that her daughter should be sent to the court of France in 1548.

From this point onwards anti-English feeling declined very rapidly, while anti-French feeling came to a head. This change of attitude followed the religious persecution organized by Cardinal Beaton soon after he gained his freedom and his ascendancy over Arran. Throughout the reign of James V the church, which was in a supine condition, had been losing the respect of all classes with alarming rapidity. The poor quality of James V's ecclesiastical appointments and the financial interests which made it impossible for him to take any hand in reforming the church from within made the decline of the church's political influence in the future very certain. Cardinal Beaton was well aware of the threat of protestantism; persecution of heretics was his answer, but it was an answer doomed to failure.

Cardinal Beaton was murdered at St Andrews in May 1546, but his death did not spell immediate defeat to the Catholic and pro-French party. After Pinkie the English advantage was not followed up, and Mary of Guise gained greatly in strength through the military support sent her from France after the departure of Mary, Queen of Scots in 1548. Mary strengthened the alliance between Scotland and France by a visit to France in 1550 which paved the way for her taking over the regency from Arran. Mary became regent in 1554, and Arran was compensated with the French duchy of Châtelhérault. When Mary, Queen of Scots reached the age of sixteen in 1558 she was married to the Dauphin Francis, eldest son of Henry II. The following year Henry II died, and Mary's husband became Francis II of France, and together with Mary joint sovereign of Scotland. Nonetheless the extension of French influence over Scotland was more apparent than real. It resulted entirely from the determination of Mary of Guise to conserve a Catholic inheritance for her daughter. The last year of the regency and the opening of the reign of Mary, Queen of Scots were to show the disillusionment with France which had followed Flodden brought to its logical conclusion.

CHAPTER VI

John Knox and Mary, Queen of Scots

Ian B. Cowan

The personalities of John Knox and Mary, Queen of Scots are inextricably bound together in the folklore of history, and yet personal contact between them was confined to seven short years. During these years, Knox was always critical of the queen's policies but that criticism seldom gained political backing and the measure of this impotence can best be judged by the fact that in the combination of events following the murder of Riccio which led to the deposition of Mary, Knox was absent, first in Ayrshire, and then in England. Any part which Knox played in the downfall of Mary can thus be attributed only to the climate of opinion which Knox had created in Scotland before that event, and not to any personal participation in the overthrow of the queen.

On this score Knox himself would have expressed little doubt as he saw Mary as a queen whose sole concern was to restore catholicism, and he could thus write: 'Sche plainlie purposed to wrak the religioun within this Realme to the Roman Antichrist she hath maid her promeise, and from him sche hath taken money to uphold his pompe'. On the other side stood the forces of protestantism ably led by their self appointed champion, John Knox, who in his *History of the Reformation in Scotland* gave lasting credence to the idea that Mary lost her throne because she was a catholic queen in a protestant realm. On both points, however, this thesis may be questioned.

The extent to which the Scottish people had embraced protestantism before Mary's return to Scotland on 19 August 1561 is debatable, but as a religious movement the Reformation had clearly limited support. The major fervency was to be found on the east coast in Angus and the Mearns, Fife and Lothian, while in the west, Kyle in Ayrshire was the centre of the reformed cause. Of the towns, Dundee in which the faithful 'exceeded all the rest in zeall and boldnes' led the way but Edinburgh was much less enthusiastic, and as late as 1565 it was reported on one occasion that as many attended the mass as the protestant service.

The part which Knox played in the growth of that reformed faith was limited. Born at Haddington about 1514, he was ordained as a priest in 1536 and apparently having failed to secure a benefice, acted thereafter as a notary and tutor. Not until 1545 when he became a follower of George Wishart did Knox evince any interest in the new religious doctrines which had been evident in Scotland for almost two decades. Thereafter, although he committed himself to the reformed cause in April 1547 by joining the murderers of Cardinal Beaton in the castle of St Andrews and subsequently acting as their minister, this stage in his career was cut short when the castle fell to the French in whose galleys Knox was condemned to row until his release in early 1549. Only at this juncture, in an England which had become fully committed to protestantism after the accession of Edward VI in 1547, did Knox become prominent. Knox's interest in this period of his career, however, was largely in the country of his adoption, although as preacher at Berwick with another congregation at Newcastle, his opinions undoubtedly began to reach a fairly wide circle of his countrymen, many of whom flocked to hear him preach. A contact was thus established which, although interrupted by Knox's flight to the continent when England returned to catholicism upon the accession of Mary Tudor in 1553, was never again to be severed. Nevertheless, with the exception of a fleeting visit to Scotland in 1555–6 during the course of which he engaged the loyalty of the Scottish protestant movement, but otherwise demonstrated its inherent weakness, Knox remained on the continent until the outbreak of the Scottish Reformation in 1559. During these years, principally spent at Geneva, Knox was as much concerned with the plight of protestantism in England as in Scotland and most of his preaching was to exiled English congregations. In his writings both countries figure prominently. *The First blast of the Trumpet against the Monstrous Regiment of Women* was directed jointly against the rule of Mary Tudor in England and that of the queen regent, Mary of Guise in Scotland. Admonitions and advice were sent to protestants in both kingdoms, and in formulating a doctrine of rebellion contrary to Calvin's theory that 'one cannot resist magistrates without resisting God', Knox was not thinking of Scotland alone. In the event, however, the accession of Elizabeth in

1558 rendered such a revolution unnecessary in England, and Knox's final position was consequently reached in that year in an *Appelation to the Nobility and Estates of Scotland* in which the people's right to resist blasphemous laws to the death was clearly asserted. To preach revolution was one thing, however, to carry it out was another, and at the end of the day, the outbreak of hostilities in Scotland owed little or nothing to John Knox or his writings.

On the contrary it can be argued that the onset of the Scottish Reformation owed much more to Mary, Queen of Scots and the policies carried out in her name by her mother acting as queen regent. Mary had been born on 7/8 December 1542, and had become queen seven days later following the death of her father James V. From that moment she became a pawn in a power struggle between England and France for influence over her realm. First advantage went to the former, but following the renunication of the Treaties of Greenwich and the subsequent 'Rough Wooing' which brought about the destruction of many religious houses, the ruinous condition of which has frequently been erroneously attributed to Knox and his fellow reformers, circumstances favoured the French. With Mary's departure for France in 1548, ostensibly for her own safety, the Franco-Scottish alliance seemed more secure than ever. In the event, the queen of Scots was to remain in France for thirteen years, and this period saw the shaping of Mary's personality at a court largely under the dominance of her mother's family of Guise. Nevertheless, although Mary's adverse characteristics have frequently been attributed by her opponents to this early upbringing, her life, certainly before marriage, seems to have been a stereotyped courtly existence in which the social graces were more important than diplomatic and political intrigue.

In Scotland, during her absence the struggle between the governor, James, earl of Arran and the queen mother, Mary of Guise continued unabated, the latter's cause being strengthened after 1548 as French ascendency in Scotland slowly increased. With the replacement of the governor by Mary of Guise as regent in 1554, that influence quickly became more overt. The new regent was a skilful politician in her own right and by various stratagems, including that of temporarily tolerating incipient protestantism in order to assure herself of the support of the burghs in which that movement was strong, she gradually outmanoeuvred all her political and religious opponents. Nevertheless, in the last resort she relied heavily upon France. French troops garrisoned Scottish castles and French administrators advised the queen regent to a point to which Scotland could be regarded as a province of France. Matters came to a head in 1558 with the marriage of the dauphin and Mary for not only was Francis given the crown matrimonial but also, in spite of promises that the kingdom should revert to the legal heirs if no child was born of the marriage, Mary signed three documents assigning her kingdom in this event to the king of France. It was those circumstances, coupled with the growing rest-lessness of the Scottish nobility who were losing all influence within their own kingdom, which principally brought the lords to take up arms against their queen in 1559.

This revolutionary outbreak was not entirely unpremeditated, however, for as early as 1557 a 'Godlie Band or Covenant' had been subscribed by a number of the Scots lords, who had also envisaged inviting Knox to return to Scotland. In the event, Knox was stopped at Dieppe, but the connection between the political motivation which was largely the mainspring of the revolution, and the religious vindication which Knox and his fellow protestants could confer upon it, was already evident. When the hour of action finally approached, Knox was again invited to return in November 1558 and with his arrival at Leith on 2 May 1559, the revolu-tionaries who had earlier got off to a somewhat uncertain start were able to proceed with a new justification.

The commitment of the lords themselves to the purpose must always remain doubtful. Some were undoubtedly genuinely protestant, but others may have been swayed in that direction by other factors. Not least amongst these were economic interests for lords and lairds alike, who had increasingly conspired to secularise the lands of the old church and who may have seen their final tenurial security in religious change which would sweep away the existing church and any claim which it might make upon its former lands and revenues. Other tangible advantages linking the political revolution with incipient protestantism stemmed from the considerable accession of physical strength, especially from the burghs, which might be expected as a result of this identification. Knox himself, moreover, with his gift of preaching, which he most effectively demonstrated in St John's Kirk in Perth, could be utilised to engage the sympathies of the populace at large. If on occasion, the resultant enthusiasm brought about the destruction of religious buildings as at Scone, Stirling and Linlithgow, Knox appears to have accepted the inevitability of such action, although he himself was far from condoning it. Even with the support of 'the rascal multitude' and the advantages of combining religious and political forces, success was by no means assured. Without a measure of good fortune which included a political crisis in France which prevented reinforcements being sent to Scotland, the death of Mary of Guise and above all the decision of Elizabeth of England to intervene, the Scots lords would have been hard pressed to sustain their challenge to the authority of the crown.

Even when that victory had been achieved, difficulties remained. In the absence of Mary, any solution could only be tentative, and as a result the main settlement – the Treaty of Edinburgh (1560) was essentially a peace treaty between France and England whereby each country agreed to withdraw its forces and the French on their part recognised Elizabeth's title, an admission which became a barrier to any ratification of the treaty by Mary. In addition certain concessions were made to the Scots, including authority to call a parliament, but with the reservation that all religious questions were to be submitted to the 'intention and pleasure' of the king and queen. In the event the lords did not abide by these conditions and the 'Reformation Parliament', which somewhat irregularly included many lairds, accepted the Scots Confession of Faith, declared the mass illegal and abrogated any authority derived from Rome. Concessions stopped short at this point, however, and there was no statutory recognition of the Reformed Church as such.

Ostensibly this was to remain the measure of Knox's success for many years thereafter, and these concessions were permanently at risk as Mary consistently refused to ratify those statutes. Moreover, the ambitious programme of the reformers for the polity and endowment of their church, the *Great Book of Reformation*, usually styled the *First Book of Discipline*, was dismissed as a book of 'devout imaginations', and no effort was made to dismiss existing benefice holders. The secular interests which had contributed to the success of a protestant Reformation thereafter conspired against it. Family connections, including that of the leader of the Lords of the Congregation, the duke of Châtelherault whose half-brother was archbishop of St Andrews, were more important than any loyalty to the Reformed Church, which in its hour of triumph had to compromise as best it could. In organisation a general assembly, mirroring in its composition the estates of the realm, had to deputise for the godly sovereign whom Knox for one would have welcomed as head of the church, while a mixture of superintendents, reformed bishops and comissioners of the assembly had to administer the church regionally instead of the godly bishops who should have replaced the existing incumbents. No decision of the *First Book of Discipline* has engendered more controversy than the expedient which would have placed the organisation of the church in the hands of superintendents, but contemporary evidence would appear to indicate that, either the office was to be permanent, or regarded as temporary pending succession to the bishoprics. Knox himself does not appear to have objected to the office as such, and his later objections to bishops in place of superintendents, appears to have arisen from his doubts as to the suitability of the proposed holders of the dignity, rather than from any antipathy to the office itself, to the restoration of which he eventually agreed in 1572. Only at congregational level did the reformers' organisation plans meet with more immediate success, as albeit slowly, kirk sessions came into being. In endowment likewise compromise was the only solution, and the Reformed Church was forced to share with the crown, one third of the taxable wealth of benefices of the old church. If the Reformation was a conspicuous political success, clearly from a protestant viewpoint, it left much to be desired.

Nevertheless, the magnitude of Knox's achievement should not be overlooked. He had successfully carried through a protestant Reformation although three short years before, this had appeared to be an unrealisable ideal. He had done so by attaching the religious aspirations of his followers to the political ambitions of the Scots lords who were prepared to accept protestantism as part of their programme in return for the material and spiritual advantages which Knox and the protestants were able to offer to them. If the reward conferred by the victorious nobles was less than just, the commitment to protestantism had been honoured. In this respect Knox's manoeuvres were highly successful, and it is as a victorious political revolutionary that he should be remembered first and foremost. Moreover, if Knox's programme thereafter met less success than it deserved, the views of the *First*

Book of Discipline, of which Knox was the principal compiler, long remained in the fields of education and social relief, the ideals which the church strove to realise. If, on the other hand, the views of Knox on church organisation were to be supplanted by those of Andrew Melville and his fellow presbyterians, it was the ideals of Knox which were to shape the beliefs and attitude towards worship adopted by the church. In this respect the Scots Confession of Faith complemented by the sections of the *Book of Discipline* dealing with worship and belief constitutes a permanent memorial to Knox. At one fell swoop a new radical Calvinism which would only accept usages and belief which were grounded in Scripture, replaced the beliefs of many centuries. The seven sacraments were reduced to two – communion and baptism which were only rightfully ministered when conjoined with public preaching. The private celebration of either sacrament was totally banned and communion was to be administered sitting around a table in the manner of the Last Supper. Kneeling to receive the communion elements which were to be administered in both kinds, was to be abandoned, as to do so implied the real presence in the elements, and as transubstantiation had been condemned, to kneel before bread and wine was idolatry. The radical break with the past did not stop short at this point, church festivals, including Christmas and Easter, were declared 'utterlie to be abolischet' on the grounds that the days set apart for such remembrance had no assurance in Scripture and the events which they commemorated were of such importance that they should be remembered throughout the whole Christian year and not only at one season. Even the concept of a valid ministry was re-interpreted and examination as to fitness and worthiness, followed by a call to preach, as Knox himself had been called at St Andrews in 1547, was all that was deemed necessary. The idea of an Apostolic succession was firmly rejected on the grounds that 'the mirakle is ceassed', and with this statement above all, Knox gave birth to a new Reformed Church, in which continuity of a sort is only discernible in the retention of certain administrative processes derived from the old church, and most notably in the figure of the 'godly bishop' or superintendent, who, bereft of any special spiritual powers, could be fittingly described as a 'pseudobishop'. In the creation of such a church, whose views were to be assailed, but never seriously threatened until more recent times, lay the abiding triumph of Knox and his fellow reformers.

This verdict, however, is necessarily given in retrospect. Without our advantage of hindsight, Knox could not be certain that victory in his terms had been won. Faced with an unsatisfactory financial settlement and denied full statutory recognition, Knox's constant fear was that of a successful counter-reformation. These fears were intensified when in December 1560, Francis II died and the realisation that Mary would return to Scotland had to be faced. Mary returned in August 1561 and thereafter for Knox the confrontation between the two Churches was symbolised in the conflict between Mary and himself. At a personal level this confrontation was certainly more symbolic than real as the number of direct clashes between Mary and Knox were few, and while in the pages of his *History*, it is Knox who emerges triumphant from these interviews, the one-sided nature of the evidence must be borne in mind as must the fact that Mary, who was every inch of six foot tall, seldom showed herself to be lacking in personal courage. On the reverse side of the coin, moreover, Knox could show himself singularly unwilling to risk the wrath of his queen as is demonstrated by his absence from Edinburgh in the closing fifteen months of her reign. In the years before this, moreover, Knox had become politically isolated from most of his former allies, who unlike himself, were prepared to compromise with their queen. Thus while Knox attacked the queen's mass from the pulpit the protestant nobility decided to acquiesce in Mary's wishes in this respect. Isolation and political impotence heightened Knox's fears of a catholic revival, but were these fears justified? Was Mary an ardent catholic and did she at any point attempt to restore catholicism in Scotland?

The key to Mary's attitude can be determined at the moment of her arrival as she made no attempt to join forces in the northeast with the pro-catholic earl of Huntly but instead landed at Leith and aligned herself with the party of Lord James Stewart and William Maitland of Lethington both of whom were politically committed to the protestant cause. Thereafter, while fair promises continued to be made to the papacy whom she assured she would be prepared to die rather than to abandon her religion, the last four years of her reign saw little indication or any attempt to aid her co-religionists beyond extending personal protection to some. Nevertheless, if Mary did not actively seek to promote catholicism, the door was always open to such a change insofar as Mary refused to officially countenance the Reformed Church and the Treaty of Edinburgh and the religious actions of the Reformation Parliament failed to gain ratification. This failure, however, sprang from political considerations outwith the realm and internally Mary was to act on more than one occasion as though the statutes had the force of law. Thus while the act forbidding the saying of the mass remained unratified, a proclamation of the privy council with similar intent was frequently acted upon. Mary showed herself equally willing, moreover, to accept the idea that power previously exercised by the Pope had passed to the crown, and this theory was acted upon in nominations to benefices and the confirmation of sales of church lands. If such actions in themselves do not fully reveal Mary's attitude to catholicism in Scotland, this was demonstrated in a more positive fashion by the part which Mary played in the downfall of the principal catholic noble in the realm, the earl of Huntly, at the battle of Corrichie in 1562. Principal responsibility for this action, which was occasioned by the need to curtail the activities of an all powerful noble, must lie with Mary and not with Lord James Stewart who although he became earl of Moray as a result of the affair, could not have successfully carried through such an expedition without the queen's approval.

In making this decision Mary demonstrated that political realities were more important than religious loyalties, and this self-same trait can be seen again and again in the queen's actions. This attitude is also seen in the fact that while she refused to recognise the Protestant Church she accepted in 1562 a measure of financial compromise by which the Reformed Church should be maintained from a general taxation of the benefices of the old church. By this arrangement two-thirds of their former revenues were left with the old incumbents, and the remaining one-third was to be collected by the government for allocation between itself and the reformed ministry. In this arrangement, practical financial considerations, particularly those of the crown itself seem to have been uppermost and other actions reveal a similar purpose. Mary's attitude towards her co-religionists was at best therefore fairly lukewarm, and as a result by 1565 communication between herself and the papacy had almost come to an end. In these circumstances, it is hardly surprising that Knox's rantings against Moray went largely unheeded, especially since Mary's policy of religious com-

G

promise was complemented by one of similar political designs in which, guided by Moray and Maitland, she ruled her protestant kingdom with apparent skill.

Mary's reign until 1565 can therefore be described with some justification as a conspicuous success, but within two years total failure had ensued and the queen had been forced to abdicate. This change in fortune can be explained in varying ways, but clearly explanations couched in religious terms have little to commend them for although Mary on the eve of her marriage to Henry, Lord Darnley, shows herself more willing to aid catholicism than at any time before, the condoning of a catholic evensong in Edinburgh coupled with other slight indications of a shift in policy, probably meant no more than a contemplation of a relaxation of the law against mass-mongering. Whatever Mary's motives, political reaction to her marriage made further concessions impossible, and as her personal position became more precarious, Mary revealed the extent to which her religious zeal was tempered by political reality when faced with the complete collapse of her policies she began in 1566 to show further favour to the Reformed Church whereby succession to lesser benefices was assured and a degree of statutory recognition achieved. Even Mary's personal devotion to catholicism, hitherto irreproachable, was seriously weakened at this juncture and after her marriage to Bothwell according to the protestant form of service, it is scarcely surprising that the Pope declared it was not his intention to have any further dealings with Mary 'unless in times to come he shall see better sign of her life and religion than he has witnessed in the past'.

Mary's fall from catholic grace through her failure to promote catholicism, or at least to maintain her personal faith, did not contribute to her fall from power. Indeed had she followed the course which so deeply distressed her catholic friends at an earlier period in her career, her position as queen of Scots might have been assured. Other reasons must therefore be sought for the cause of Mary's downfall and while arguments based upon her femininity and defects of character cannot be entirely dismissed they have little to commend them. Mary was certainly not helpless as her actions before the battle of Corrichie attest, as does similarly the resolution with which she acted against the opponents of her marriage to Darnley when in chasing them over the border, it was reported that 'the queen's courage increased man-like, so much, that she was ever with the foremost'. Mary's downfall therefore cannot be easily attributed to feminine frailty in moments of political stress. Likewise arguments based upon her sexuality and passionate nature tend to overlook the fact that neither of her Scottish marriages were simple cases of infatuation. Both had sound political advantages to commend them. As her husband, Darnley's own claim to the English throne would strengthen her own, while as the bridegroom's mother, Lady Lennox, if not Darnley himself, was a staunch catholic, such a match would be to the liking of other catholic powers and the Pope. Above all, however, Mary may have hoped with Darnley as king, for an extension of the personal power which she had hitherto lacked. These advantages and the disadvantages of the match, the displeasure of Elizabeth, the wrath of the nobility and that of Knox and the church all appear to have been seriously weighed before the final decision was taken, and even then there was no precipitate rush towards the marriage bed until political expediency dictated otherwise. If in her later marriage to James Hepburn, earl of Bothwell, passion can be more readily discerned, it is also clear that political reliance upon the earl, which had increased as Mary realised that her husband was an ineffectual drunkard, became a matter of complete necessity, for which Mary was prepared to sacrifice her religious beliefs, following upon the murder of Darnley.

Neither passion, nor religious fanaticism brought about the downfall of Mary. Politics alone was at the heart of the matter, and such considerations appear always to have been Mary's prime motivation. In the period immediately following upon her return to Scotland her policies appear to have been directed towards gaining recognition as Elizabeth's heir, although it is equally possible that the conviction expressed in 1558 that she was rightful queen of England never quite deserted her. The refusal to ratify the Treaty of Edinburgh, which would have entailed recognising Elizabeth's title points in this direction, as does the search for a powerful continental suitor, who as her husband, could help her implement her claims. Elizabeth's only weapon in this fray, the promise that if Mary married to please her, she would be made her heir, was clearly ineffectual if Mary could find a powerful husband who would help her implement her immediate claim. For three years the two queens and their ministers parried with one another on this issue with the final advantage eventually resting with Elizabeth, who when it became evident that Mary could not find a continental suitor, announced that she would not name her heir. Mary at this juncture faced the choice of a future devoid of political significance with increasing dependence upon the policies of Moray and Maitland, or of attempting to exert her personal influence to a far greater point than hitherto. The prerequisite for the latter course was marriage, but unfortunately Mary's choice, Darnley, was unpleasing to the nobility and the church. Nevertheless, her resolute actions after her marriage bear the hallmark of a queen enjoying real political power for the first time. For multifarious reasons this advantage proved transitory, and in order to retrieve a situation which Mary increasingly blamed on the ineffectiveness of her husband, new advisers were required.

Outwith the ranks of the nobility, David Riccio, the queen's French secretary, became a close confidante, so much so, that a hostile nobility and a jealous husband conspired in his murder before their pregnant queen on 9 March 1566. Mary's resolution in the circumstances was praiseworthy, and the guilty nobles followed in turn by Knox, who does not seem to have been implicated in the murder, but evidently feared the queen's wrath, left Edinburgh shortly after the event. The incident not only confirmed Mary in her loathing of her husband, but increased her sense of isolation. At this juncture Mary's principal desire appears to have been to rid herself of Darnley while her greatest need was a new and powerful ally. The latter condition was met by Bothwell, but whether he conspired to grant her other wish will always remain a mystery. If Bothwell remains the chief suspect in the actual slaying of Darnley, and he certainly appears to have been involved in the mining of Kirk o' Field if not in the actual strangulation of the fleeing Darnley, Mary's part in the affair also continues to be a matter of debate. However, this much remains clear : Mary made no secret of the fact that she wished to be rid of her husband, and it was she who delivered him into the hands of his enemies by bringing him from Glasgow to Edinburgh. Various reasons have been advanced for this, including the thesis that Mary was pregnant by Bothwell and wished to hide her moral shortcomings. It is much more likely, however, that political realities rather than morality governed Mary's actions at this juncture, and having prepared the scene, no further action was required on her part but to await the *dénouement*. With the deed accomplished, Mary, however, found herself no freer than before, and Bothwell, supposedly her husband's slayer, previously a useful asset, thereafter became politically indispensable. It was, however, this political alignment with Bothwell, and not her adulterous affair with the earl, which caused the nobility to take to arms. Lack of morality might in retrospect be sufficient grounds for deposing a queen, and hence the importance of the Casket Letters which were later produced to justify this point of view, but it required a political opposition to effect such a deposition. Mary's mistakes on this occasion were irretrievable, and defeat at Carberry on 15 June 1567 was followed a month later by enforced abdication in favour of her one year old son James.

Ten days after her surrender to the victorious lords, Knox returned to Edinburgh to gloat over his fallen rival, and preach at the coronation of her son in the parish church of Stirling on 29 July 1567. Ironically, however, the factors surrounding Mary's eclipse also encompassed Knox, for following Mary's escape from Lochleven castle in 1568, subsequent defeat at Langside and flight to England, successive Scottish regents found it necessary to placate Mary's captor Elizabeth to whom Knox remained completely unacceptable. Political impotence, coupled with ill-health, meant that while in the years before his death in 1572 his considerable reputation brought to him the veneration owing to an elder statesman of the Kirk, few listened to his words of advice or admonition. Nevertheless, his place in the annals of history was assured and lest there be any doubt on that score he left behind him his *History of the Reformation of Religion within the Realm of Scotland,* not only a masterpiece of language and style and an important historical source, but also a superb autobiography which has largely contributed to posterity's view of Knox and the part which he played in the Reformation movement. If, however, the traditional view of Knox was somewhat shaped by the pen rather than by deed, his great rival Mary Stewart was not to be outdone in that respect. If few, even of her more avid contemporary supporters wished to dwell upon the events of her reign in Scotland, her prolonged captivity and final execution in England allowed her to pose, and be presented as a champion of catholicism. Her real aims and intentions, however, were probably consistent with her earlier ambitions, as even in captivity Elizabeth's throne appears to have been her principal objective. Her plotting at this stage of her career was as inept in England as it had been in Scotland, and she paid the price accordingly. At the end, however, she played to perfection the martyr's role for which she had already been cast by her champions, and thus achieved an immortality which her struggle with Knox alone could not have conferred upon her.

CHAPTER VII

James VI and Vanishing Frontiers

Gordon Donaldson

One of the few historical facts which has almost universal currency is that James VI of Scotland became king of England, and even Scots who should know better too often call him 'James the First'. But the genealogical accident which took him to the English throne is not the most important fact about the sixth James. His accession to England saw the disappearance of the frontier at the historic Border, but within Scotland itself he eliminated other frontiers – between political and ecclesiastical parties, between different ways of life and even different races – and welded his countrymen into a unified kingdom of which he was the unquestioned head.

The prospect of such achievements was remote indeed when he was crowned at the age of thirteen months. He had been raised to the throne by a mere faction among the nobles, and civil war against his mother's supporters went on for six years. The first regent, the earl of Moray, never conciliated the Hamiltons, who favoured the deposed Mary, and it was by a Hamilton that he was murdered in 1570. His successor the earl of Lennox, Darnley's father, was also murdered, in an affray arising from the war with the Marian Party in 1571. The third regent, the earl of Mar, was no more able than his predecessors to restore tranquillity to the distracted country before he died after thirteen months in office – it is said of a broken heart because he loved peace and could not attain it. The fourth, the earl of Morton, ruled until 1580, but even then the king was only fourteen and the great families returned happily to their custom of competing among themselves for the direction of affairs. The period since Flodden in 1513 had been one in which there were three minorities – of James V, of Mary and of James VI – so that in the space of more than seventy years there were no more than twenty-two years of rule by a monarch of mature age.

The old problems of curbing the nobility and extending law and order, which had exercised kings for generations, were intensified by new problems arising from the Reformation. Dissension between those who supported protestantism and the English alliance and those who stood by Rome and the traditional alliance with France exacerbated ancient feuds. Active or militant Roman Catholicism was hardly significant, if only because of the dearth of priests, but there was much latent sympathy with catholicism in certain areas, and no one could have predicted how much support a skilfully led Roman Catholic revival might have enjoyed. This problem was tied up with that of the king's mother, who was also his rival and who lived, though in captivity in England, through the first twenty years of James's reign.

There was another problem which arose from the Reformation. In Scotland the Protestant Church had been set up not on royal initiative but as the outcome of two revolutions – one in 1560 against the Queen Mother, Mary of Guise, and the second, in 1567, against Queen Mary herself. It is true that the protestants professed their readiness to accept the rule of a 'godly prince' in the person of James, and a new generation might become reconciled to royal control over the church, but it was not going to be easy to shake off the tradition of ecclesiastical independence. The Reformed Church had developed its general assembly, comprising the same elements which formed a parliament – any nobles who cared to attend, lairds representing the shires and burgesses chosen by town councils, alongside a number of ministers. Thus parliament, as well as the king, had a rival, and the assembly was an admirable platform for any militant faction.

Such a faction arose in the shape of the presbyterian movement. Initially the Reformed Church had had a quasi-episcopal constitution, with superintendents and other individual overseers, and in 1572 it was decided, with general approval, that the crown should appoint ministers to bishoprics; these bishops would sit in parliament, exercise the functions of superintendents and be subject to the general assembly in spiritual matters. This arrangement was challenged by Andrew Melville, who returned to Scotland in 1574, after five years at Geneva, to become principal first at Glasgow University and then at St Mary's College, St Andrews. A logical thinker with no notion of tact, diplomacy or expediency, Melville argued that, as all ministers were equal, power should not lie with bishops or superintendents but with committees or courts, expecially presbyteries. This in itself meant that it would no longer be open to the crown to influence the church through bishops, but Melville went further in his application of the doctrine that church and state formed 'Two Kingdoms'. Laymen in the commonly accepted sense of the term were to be wholly excluded from ecclesiastical government : barons and burgesses were no longer to attend the general assembly unless they happened to be elders, and crown and parliament were to have no authority over the church. But Melville did not propose a reciprocal exclusion of ministers from power in the state, for God was the Head of both Kingdoms and the ministers could 'teach the magistrate how the civil jurisdiction should be exercised according to the Word'. One minister told the king 'There is a judgment above yours, and that is God's, put in the hand of the ministry, for we shall judge the angels, saith the Apostle'. This meant the rule of a clerical oligarchy in the shape of the majority in the general assembly.

With so many disturbing elements in church and state, there were ample grounds for the growth of factions, founded partly on principles and partly, as ever, on personal and family feuds. The traditions of Queen Mary's party were inherited by what may be called broadly a conservative faction, sympathetic to proposals for Mary's restoration, favourable to Roman Catholicism or to episcopacy, and anxious for the alignment of Scotland with France or Spain. The existence of this group constantly aroused hopes among Roman Catholic agents that Scotland could be rallied to the papal cause as a base for a crusade against heretical England. On the other side was an ultra-protestant faction, hostile to Mary and anyone else tainted with 'papistry' and eager for the alliance of Scotland with England against the Romanist powers of the continent. This faction gave some countenance to the presbyterian ministers, who for their part used their pulpits for propaganda in favour of an English alliance and against Rome. This party was also hand-in-glove with the English puritan politicians who were always trying to divert Elizabeth's foreign policy into an anti-Catholic crusade.

Morton, the fourth regent, was a good friend to England and had no place in his government for former supporters of Mary. He was equally a good friend to episcopacy but, although he censured Mclville, he took no action to prevent the growth of the presbyterian party, and, although he questioned the legality of the general assembly, he did not suppress it. In 1578 the assembly adopted Melville's proposals and went on to condemn the office of bishop. This in itself was bound to lead to a clash with the state, for the place of bishops in ecclesiastical administration, as well as much else that Melville wanted to sweep away, was founded on statute law; the assembly could proclaim a programme, but only parliament could put it into effect. If Morton did nothing to check the presbyterian threat, he did nothing, either, to prevent the growth of a faction opposed to him, and he neglected to ingratiate himself with the young king. James was being brought up in Stirling Castle, where the dominant figure in his education was George Buchanan, an elderly academic and a stern disciplinarian who thought it his duty to instil into his pupil a hatred of his mother as an adulteress and a murderess, to drill him in classical scholarship and to indoctrinate him with concepts of constitutional monarchy; Buchanan did much to shape and perhaps to warp James's personality, but the king, when he grew to manhood, was to reject many of his tutor's lessons.

After Morton's fall, in 1580, rival factions in turn seized power in a series of *coups d'état*. The king, now fourteen, gave his adolescent devotion to an accomplished cousin from France, Esmé Stewart, and created him duke of Lennox. There is little reason to believe that Lennox had any real interest in either the revival of Roman Catholicism or the restoration of Mary, but he was regarded with wild optimism by Roman Catholic agents and with equal suspicion by the presbyterians, whom he defied by making a fresh appointment to the archbishopric of Glasgow. A reaction came in 1582, when a party of ultra-protestant lords, led by William Ruthven, earl of Gowrie, seized the king's person in the Ruthven Raid and formed an administration which lasted for ten months. They tried to reach a firm understanding with Elizabeth and they allowed the presbyterians to develop their organisation, though still without statutory authority. When the king escaped from the Ruthven Raiders, Lennox was dead, but an administration was formed under James Stewart, created earl of Arran, who brought back into office some former Marians and other conservatives who had been excluded under Morton. This government passed the 'Black Acts' which reaffirmed episcopal government and made it plain that supremacy over the church was to rest with the crown-in-parliament, and it drove Andrew Melville and many of his followers, as well as the lords who had taken part in the Ruthven Raid, into exile in England. At the end of 1585 the exiled lords returned from England in force and overthrew Arran.

By this time James was nineteen and his own views began to influence policy. In one of his earliest pronouncements he declared his intention to be a 'universal king', not the agent of a faction but able to choose his ministers at his pleasure. Not a strong party man by temperament, he aimed at a *via media* to which he could reconcile the majority – he hoped all – of his people. His material interests also prompted him to take this line. One objective was to succeed Elizabeth, and this inclined him to favour the protestantism which was maintained in England. At the same time, he was aware of the strength of English Roman Catholicism, and there was a possibility that Spain might intervene either before or at Elizabeth's death and re-establish a Roman ascendancy. If, therefore, James maintained an equivocal policy he would commend himself to English Roman Catholics and perhaps even succeed to England under papal auspices. Besides, he had always a prudential regard for his own safety, and to show himself an intransigent protestant might encourage the pope to authorise a fanatical Jesuit to assassinate him.

An attempt to maintain a balance between the rival Scottish parties was made after Arran's fall in 1585, for the government which was then formed was a kind of coalition, in which men who had been in office under Arran were retained alongside ultra-protestants. At the head of it was John Maitland of Thirlestane, himself a former Marian and the brother of Mary's secretary, William Maitland of Lethington, but shrewd enough to see the importance of keeping on good terms with England and with the presbyterians. A league with England was concluded in 1586, accompanied by an English pension for James and an assurance that Elizabeth would not oppose his claims to the English throne unless he provoked her. Such strong inducements to good behaviour went far to ensure James's acquiescence in his mother's execution in 1587 and his neutrality when the Spanish Armada sailed in 1588. The league with England pleased the presbyterians and ultra-protestants and reduced their political force, for they were no longer likely to act as English agents, and it was safe to make concessions to them. In 1586 an attempt was made to combine presbyterian and episcopalian elements in the church system, but when this proved unacceptable to the presbyterians they were tacitly permitted to go ahead with the unofficial development of their organisation. Simultaneously, the bishops were deprived of the bulk of their properties, and the result was a temporary eclipse of episcopacy.

The political force of the contrary faction was reduced by Mary's execution, for their plotting could now have only the un-patriotic aim of assisting Spain to conquer Britain. The earls of Huntly, Errol and Crawford in the north-east and Lord Maxwell in the south-west were active enough in communicating with Philip of Spain, but they seem to have been uncertain of their objectives and had little support beyond the bounds of their own family and territorial influence. It seemed safe enough for the government to follow its policy of conciliation by refraining from strong measures against them. The difficulty was that leniency to the 'popish earls', as they were called, infuriated the presbyterians and went a long way to nullify the concessions to them. On the other hand, acquiescence in the progress of presbyterianism nullified the pretence that the king looked favourably on the cause of Rome.

It must have become evident that conciliation all round was as yet premature. To be a 'universal king', superior to faction, re-quired force or money or diplomacy. As James had neither money nor men at his disposal, coercion was impossible, but he had an ample stock of tactical skill. There is no direct evidence of the trend of his thought, but the necessary inference is that he decided to lean on the presbyterians until he had destroyed the political danger of the Roman Catholic faction. In 1592 an act of parlia-ment officially authorised the presbyterian system of church govern-ment. The measure did not amount to what Andrew Melville had asked, for it did not concede ecclesiastical independence, the office of bishop was not abolished and nothing was done for the endow-ment of the Reformed Church. James's amiability cost little in political, and nothing in financial, terms, but with the support of the ultra-protestants he was now able to put pressure on the northern earls to abandon their intrigues with Spain, and Andrew Melville accompanied a royal army which marched against them. They showed that, while they would intrigue and bluster and even raise armed forces, they would not face the king in the field. They were forced to go abroad in 1595 and at last made a formal sub-mission to both parliament and assembly in 1596.

This menace being removed, it was time to turn on the presbyterians, and the king did this with a rapidity which makes the conclusion inescapable that his moves had been planned.

Events played into his hands. The presbyterians had been involved in politics since at least as far back as the Ruthven Raid, when they gave their blessing to that 'act of reformation' as they called it. More recently, they had taken up the cause of 'the bonnie Earl o' Moray' (son-in-law of the earl of Moray who had earlier been the darling of the protestants). Despite the moving ballad, which presents Moray as 'the queen's true love', his murder by the earl of Huntly was the outcome only of a long-standing feud between two nobles who supported rival policies, but James had a personal preference for Huntly and refused to punish him as the presbyterians demanded. Another troublesome peer whom the ministers favoured was Francis Stewart, earl of Bothwell, nephew of Mary's Bothwell. Francis gained notoriety by his alleged resort to witchcraft to raise storms when the king sailed to Denmark in 1589 to bring home his bride and by repeatedly forcing his way into the royal presence with no other apparent aim than to demonstrate the king's lack of power. James was ready enough to believe in the seriousness of the witch cults which seem to have been common at the time, but in his timid and cautious soul he may also have had a reluctant admiration for Bothwell's dash and verve. However, Bothwell, besides being at feud with Maitland of Thirlestane, endeared himself to the ministers by leading the opposition to the king's leniency to Huntly and the other 'popish earls', and some presbyterians acclaimed him as a 'a sanctified plague' who would make the king 'turn to God'. Ministers were not content with rebuking the king for his personal behaviour, but persisted in trying to interfere in both domestic and foreign policy and over-reached themselves. Andrew Melville addressed James as 'God's silly vassal' and one of his colleagues characterised all kings as 'devil's children'. A rather mysterious riot in Edinburgh at the end of 1596 was represented by the king as an illustration of the danger of clerical power, and he turned it to account to bring Edinburgh to grovelling submission and to secure for himself a voice in the selection of ministers for the leading towns.

From 1596–7, when the political dangers from both Roman Catholic and presbyterian factions were effaced, the king passed from defence to attack. He used a remarkable range of devices to revive episcopacy. He could appoint a minister to the title of a bishopric; the general assembly could appoint a minister as visitor of a district and could decide that presbyteries and synods should have 'constant moderators' or permanent chairmen; parliament could restore to the bishops the bulk of their revenues. All these things were done, and when a minister who held the title and revenues of a bishopric acted as visitor of his diocese and was constant moderator of the synod he began to look very like a bishop. In 1610 the general assembly gave its approval to an episcopal constitution. This success was not achieved without a certain amount of characteristic trickery. The general assembly approved at first only of constant moderators of presbyteries, but the king, by the simple device of falsifying the minutes, made out that the approval extended to synods as well. Similarly, when parliament in 1612 ratified the restoration of episcopacy the assembly's minutes had again been falsified, for certain limitations on the powers of bishops were omitted.

James could not have proceeded so far without taming the general assembly. Melville's influence had depended on the support of the majority of the ministers who regularly attended the assembly, but as it always met in the south hardly any of the more conservative ministers from the north turned up. However, the act of 1592, which authorised the assembly, had given the king the power to name its place of meeting, and James began to name places like Montrose and Aberdeen, where the radicals would not swamp the house. He also exploited his power to fix the date of meeting. When he advanced the pre-arranged date, no one could object, and he then went on to defer it. In 1605, when some ministers insisted on constituting an assembly after the king had postponed it, they were successfully prosecuted. Then Andrew Melville and some other leading militants were summoned to London, ostensibly for a conference, and were not allowed to return to Scotland. For the remainder of the reign, while assemblies might be restive, they were never defiant. The king's power to legislate for the church had been acknowledged by parliament in 1606, but James, who remarked with characteristic shrewdness that 'prerogative is a secret which ryves (tears) in the stretching', preferred to work by constitutional means. Whereas episcopacy had been reaffirmed by parliament in 1584 and presbytery authorised by parliament in 1592, he dexterously arranged that in 1610 a general assembly (containing equitable representation from the whole country) passed the acts to restore episcopacy.

It was not only because of the king's severity towards the

presbyterian leaders that his changes in church government were accepted. The ministers were vocal, but they had little power in themselves. They might perhaps try to stir up the people, but the changes in church government made little difference to the every-day working of the church: kirk sessions continued to operate, and the bishops actually increased their numbers and effectiveness; and presbyteries still met to carry out their functions without much reference to the bishops. Consequently, there was little that the ordinary worshipper could disapprove of, if he noticed any change at all. It was perhaps more important that, as Scottish society was largely dominated by the nobles, if the king could appease them he could disregard ministers and people alike. Now, nobles who had acquired church property had no taste for the financial proposals of Melville, who claimed all ecclesiastical revenues for the Reformed Church and denounced the diversion of any of them to laymen as sacrilege. Besides, the Reformation had transferred to the crown the control of church property, and this made the nobles dependent on the king for the transformation of their rights in church lands into hereditary holdings and for grants of additional lands. Wise kings had always used patronage to gain support, and now the king had at his disposal patronage on an unparalleled scale.

While there is thus some truth in the statement that James bought the nobles with the lands of the monasteries, there were other elements in his dealings with them. His assertion of the divine right of his kingship was the necessary answer, framed by a king who was himself a theologian, to the claims of the presbyterians that he was answerable to the ministers. James did not deny that he was God's vassal, and indeed rather gloried in the fact, but he believed in One Kingdom, comprising both church and state, of which he was the earthly head, without the need for ministers as intermediaries. Yet he was far too shrewd to obtrude his dignity in his day to day dealings with his subjects. Divine right meant that James had always a strong sense of his responsibilities, and he remarked sagely that 'the highest bench is slidderiest (most slippery) to sit upon'. Besides, while he dogmatised about divine right, he had an easy familiarity with nobles and commons alike which took the sting out of his dogmatising and gave him oppor-tunities to use his undoubted gifts of cajolery. The earl of Mar was 'Jockie o' the sclates' because, when he had shared James's schooling, he had shown a marked ability in arithmetic. The earl of Haddington was 'Tam o' the Cowgate', from his place of residence in Edinburgh. Moreover, James had not studied both contemporary Scotland and Scottish history without learning that conciliation paid better dividends than severity. He preferred to avoid head-on collisions, and there were few executions or forfeitures.

Yet, while James conciliated the nobles, he did not depend much on them for the conduct of administration. He declared at one stage that he would not use great men to manage his affairs, but only 'such as he could correct and were hangable'. The 'hangable' men on whom he relied – and none of whom he ever hanged – were younger sons of noble houses or men of middle-class origin. Maitland of Thirlestane himself was the first chancellor in the century who was neither a prelate nor a peer, and on Maitland's fall James at once selected ministers who were to serve him well throughout the rest of his reign. His bishops, too, were middle-class administrators who served in the state as well as the church.

Frontiers between political factions, frontiers between parties in the church, were going down, and frontiers between feuding noble families followed them, according to the design of a king who had a marked distaste for bloodshed and even for the sight of arms – possibly, it has been suggested, because of ante-natal experience, when the daggers of Riccio's murderers flashed before his mother's eyes three months before his birth. After the riot in Edinburgh in December 1596 there was a period of unprecedented tranquillity, lasting for forty years into the reign of James's son but appropriately called 'King James's Peace'. In fact, while James's victory over the presbyterians is spectacular, the achievement which did most to shape the future of Scotland was his success in instilling a new respect for law and order. Many efforts were made to improve criminal justice, but it was characteristic that James laid the emphasis on the prevention of crime rather than its punishment, and it was for this reason that he instituted justices of the peace. They achieved relatively little, probably because the king was too cautious to invest them with powers which would have infringed the rights of the nobles' courts, and perhaps more was done through the unobtrusive but persistent efforts of the kirk sessions. The sessions constantly held up certain standards of conduct and they dealt on the spot with minor offences by word and deed which, if unchecked, could easily have led to serious crimes. In the towns the sessions worked closely with the town councils, and James himself saw clearly the parallel between the work of the sessions and the functions he proposed for his justices of the peace. At a different level, it was significant of the growing maturity of the Scottish state that James, after carrying out much-needed measures of financial reorganisation, was able to introduce to Scotland something like regular taxation. The reign also saw the institution of the Register of Sasines, which provided a unique record of all transactions in real estate. All in all, the king succeeded in making Scotland what he called 'a weill governit commonweal'.

The Scottish parliament had never developed into an effective check on a resolute king and had seldom been the scene of independent debates. James increased its representative character by introducing shire commissioners to represent lesser landowners – a measure which strengthened it against the general assembly – but he also perfected machinery which enabled him to control its proceedings and secure its acquiescence in his measures. His main instrument in ruling Scotland, especially after he went to England, was the privy council, to which he directed a stream of instructions and so governed Scotland 'through the post'. He boasted that he could rule Scotland by his pen, which others had not done by the sword.

While the government thus became more intensive, it also became more extensive, at the expense of ancient frontiers, geographical, racial and cultural. The problem of 'putting order on the Border' was one which had defeated James's predecessors. The lands on both sides of the Border had constituted something of a land apart, with its own code of behaviour; the Borderers were apt to regard Anglo-Scottish warfare as a kind of rough game in which no one should be seriously hurt, were disinclined to regard either Edinburgh or London and were able to find a refuge across the frontier when either government tried to take action. After 1603 the problem could be tackled as a joint Anglo-Scottish operation, and the Borders, now the 'Middle Shires' of James's enlarged kingdom, were disciplined by mounted police until they hardly knew themselves. In one year more than 140 of 'the nimblest and most powerful thieves in all the Borders' ended their days on the gallows.

As only the North Channel separated the western Highlands

and islands from Ireland, the situation there had been not unlike that on the Borders. After 1603 the Scottish government could collaborate with the English administration in Ulster, and James was then able to reduce the west Highlands to obedience. He put an end to the policy of raising up feudal magnates at the expense of clan chiefs, and relied instead on royal officials, including bishops, and on the clan chiefs themselves, whom he made responsible for the good behaviour of their followers. The Reformed Church was extended to the west, to bring not only the gospel but also the kirk session discipline. James was responsible, too, for the settlement of Protestant Englishmen and Lowland Scots in Ulster, in order to drive a wedge between two areas of Celtic Catholicism. The design was well-conceived, but this, James's sole experiment in creating rather than abolishing a frontier, has been a source of trouble ever since.

In Orkney and Shetland, where the earls wielded almost sovereign power, the problem was not one of too little government but – so at least the natives thought – too much government, and government by the old Norse laws, which gave the earls peculiar opportunities to demonstrate the truth of the old saying that 'justice is mighty profitable'. Once again a bishop was called in as a royal agent; Earl Patrick Stewart spent the last years of his life in prison and the Norse laws were abolished in 1611.

James's concept of One Kingdom, initially the answer to the challenge of the Reformed Church, was coming to have a wider meaning. It was fatal to the feudal, baronial or clan characteristics of Scottish society and to any deviation from the king's laws. As the various frontiers went down, it became increasingly true that there was indeed one kingdom in Scotland.

One aspect of the work of a busy and paternal government was a flow of well-intentioned economic legislation, mainly designed to restrain the export of raw materials and thereby encourage manufactures, the introduction of skilled foreigners to teach their crafts and the issue of patents for the 'projects' of various inventors. Some new industries did take root, and there is a good deal of evidence of expanding commerce, notably the export of coal and salt. However, probably less was done to bring about commercial expansion by legislation than by the new conditions of order and security. Farmers, likewise, could now sow their seed with some confidence that no human agency would prevent them from reaping their harvest, and agriculture benefited also from the widespread substitution of proprietorship for tenancies. There is ample evidence of the increasing wealth of the merchant classes and the farmers alike.

Economic improvements, added to peace and stability, were conducive to intellectual and cultural activities. Among the king's subjects were John Napier of Merchiston, the inventor of logarithms, and Timothy Pont, Scotland's first cartographer. Two universities were founded – Edinburgh in 1582 and Marischal College, Aberdeen, in 1593 – bringing Scotland's total to five. Although neither owed anything to royal initiative, a scholarly king delighted to patronise universities and he decreed that Edinburgh University should be known as 'The Academy of King James'. The number of parish schools had been increasing, and an act of the privy council in 1616 was the first measure for the maintenance of a school in every parish.

Architecture was finding new outlets. Hitherto Scottish residences, with the exception of two or three royal palaces, had been essentially fortified places, castles or tower-houses, with little adornment. Now that feuds and disturbances were falling out of fashion, defence was less necessary and, although some were reluctant to abandon their towers, if only because 'the world may change again', the utilitarian tower-house gave way to what was more like a castellated mansion. Purely domestic buildings, without pretence at fortification, also appeared, conspicuously in the palace built at Kirkwall about 1600 by the king's cousin, Earl Patrick Stewart. Another cousin, the troublesome earl of Bothwell, inserted into the courtyard of Crichton Castle a domestic range with an Italianate facade unique in Scotland. The king's own building, at Edinburgh Castle and Linlithgow Palace, represents a Jacobean style some of whose features were imitated by his subjects in their own houses. Scottish architecture was notably enriched by a style quite different from the Jacobean houses of England; there was some debt to Danish models, but also considerable independence.

If architecture thus had a vernacular character, in language and literature the trend was towards assimilation to England. The Scots never had a printed Bible in their own tongue, but depended on English versions, and the Reformed Church was an instrument in habituating them to standard English, with the result that Scots practically disappeared as a literary vehicle even before the union of the crowns. The king was himself a poet of some competence and even in the 1580s he was assembling other versifiers around him. The tradition of a courtly group of poets was continued later in the reign by William Drummond of Hawthornden and Sir William Alexander. Jacobean poetry was closely associated with the cultivation of music, in which likewise the king took an interest. Former monks and priests brought the musical skill of the old church into the service of the new; English musicians provided the music of the court; the song-schools in the burghs were maintained, and schoolboys and undergraduates had opportunities to learn vocal and instrumental music.

It is in this reign that we first find an appreciable number of portraits of Scotsmen, though the artists were often foreigners. The main outlet of painting was the mural decoration and painted ceilings of which so many specimens survive and which suggest that Scottish houses were internally a riot of colour. The detail of the work was not always of the highest quality, but the general intention to introduce gaiety and brightness is unmistakable. The subjects, occasionally scriptural, were often secular and sometimes obscene, and indicate an outlook far removed from a dismal puritanical austerity. Many churches were adorned with sepulchral monuments showing a very high standard of craftsmanship in a Renaissance style, following a fashion common in both England and Denmark.

James's accession to the English throne brought him enlarged prestige as well as immunity from the *coups d'état* which had punctuated his earlier years. But there were disadvantages. Removed from everyday contact with subjects who could presume on their familiarity to criticise him, he was surrounded instead by obsequious prelates and flattering courtiers. His ablest achievements belong to the days of his adversity before 1596, when he had to meet challenge after challenge; in the days of his prosperity he was less willing to attend to business with his old shrewdness and he lost his sureness of touch. It was remarked that the Scottish kings were like the horses of Mar, which 'in youth are good but in their old age bad'. Perhaps it was James's misfortune that he lived to be almost fifty-nine, which made him older than all the sovereigns of his house except the first two and the last.

Not content with his changes in church government, James began, from 1612 onwards, to move towards changes in worship.

There was much support for improvements, and a process of revision initiated by a general assembly at Aberdeen in 1616 produced three drafts of a new service-book. But, whereas the first and second represented Scottish tradition, the third was more like a version of the English Prayer book. Moreover, the king brought forward five other proposals: the observance of the main holy days of the Christian year; kneeling at Communion; private Communion; private Baptism; and confirmation by bishops. Changes in worship, unlike the revival of episcopacy, affected what the ordinary worshipper saw in his church Sunday by Sunday. Although grudging approval was given to the Five Articles by a general assembly at Perth in 1618, opposition was so intense, especially to kneeling at Communion, that the king, who had not lost all his common sense, saw that he must go no further. No new service-book was issued and in 1621, when parliament (again through the support of representatives from the north) approved the Five Articles, it seems that James gave an undertaking that if they were approved he would propose no more innovations. Not only did he keep his word, but his bishops were sensible enough not to press the Articles on clergy or people.

Economic prosperity no doubt helped to make men content with James's government and added to his subjects' respect for him. It was not mere flattery when one of his servants referred to 'this dilectable time of peace under your Majesty's happy reign and most excellent government'. There might be occasional grumbling, over his ecclesiastical innovations and over his taxation, but the days were to come when men would look back with regret to the 'great wisdom' of 'blessed King James'.

CHAPTER VIII

Montrose and Argyll

Edward J. Cowan

In the seamless web of history the destinies of individuals are sometimes strangely intertwined. One such strand was woven into the complex fabric of the Covenanting era in the complementary careers of James Graham, fifth earl of Montrose and Archibald Campbell, eighth earl of Argyll. Both were Covenanters and both *the Great Marquis* to their respective admirers who, exaggerating differences between them more apparent than real, transformed both into symbols which they themselves would only partially have recognised.

Born in 1612, five years Argyll's junior, James Graham was handsome, talented, and militarily gifted. He shared with Archibald Campbell a taste for mathematics, history and golf. Both were medallists in archery at St Andrews University. Montrose spent his youth on his Perthshire and Angus estates. He made frequent visits to the home of his brother-in-law, Colquhoun of Luss on Loch Lomondside, where he acquired some Gaelic and the traditional Colquhoun dislike of clan Campbell. After an excursion to the Continent in the 1630s he was presented at court but due to the venomous tongue of the marquis of Hamilton, who personally supervised the mismanagement of Scottish affairs during the following decade, he was coldly received by Charles I. His day would come. In youth the ingenuous Montrose was believed to have 'taken upon him the part of the hero too much and lived as in a romance'. He carried his romanticism to the gallows, but in his career there is an elegiac quality reminiscent of his own poetry.

In contrast the biography of Argyll can be characterised as pedestrian prose. Possessed of a well known obliquity of vision, 'gley'd eyed Archibald' appears cast by Nature in the role of villain. Charged with shiftiness, cowardice, unreliability, and a vacillating opportunism, qualities in themselves seldom incompatible with political success, his *métier* lay in intrigue rather than military endeavour. Yet there is ample testimony to his personal charm, conversational accomplishment and his 'large and understanding heart'. He was also MacCalein Mor, chief of the most powerful Highland clan, which had risen on the ruins of the Lordship of the Isles. As the instrument of crown policy the Campbells had smoked out many a 'byke of lawless limmers', including MacDonalds, MacLeans and MacGregors whose territories they promptly engrossed. Clan affairs preoccupied Argyll at Inveraray until his appointment to the privy council in 1628. His orbit remained emphatically Highland. His austere presbyterianism led to a clash with the episcopal authorities in the 1630s. He was also an early supporter of the most profound and literarily gifted of the Covenanting theorists, Samuel Rutherford.

The careers of both men have been distorted by successive historians bent on finding their own political or religious bias reflected in the age. Argyll described himself as 'a distracted man, a distracted subject of a distracted time wherein I lived'. Both he and Montrose were bewildered human beings struggling against a wave of complex forces which would eventually engulf them. Both were martyrs to the faithlessness of Charles Stewart, dying for ideals greater than themselves. Argyll, a man of his time, was undoubtedly devious. Although at his trial, for example, he strenuously denied having ordered the burning of Forther Castle in Angus, a surviving letter not only proves the contrary but contains the rider, 'you need not to let know that you have directions from me to fire it'. Montrose, also a prisoner of his age, sacked Aberdeen in 1644 and was powerless to prevent massacres of the Campbells at Inveraray and Inverlochy, had he been so inclined. Yet he was on the whole more consistent, less a politician, more a man of principle. As staunch Calvinists both subscribed to what has been called 'the thesis of progressive comprehension', namely that previous agreements or bargains (saving a covenant with God) could be made redundant by subsequent revelation. And when the wave finally broke on the rocks both died convinced of their own salvation.

The 'small cloud in the north' was expanded into a storm which engulfed England, Ireland and Scotland in civil war, largely through the folly of Charles I. The union of 1603 constituted a severe psychological blow to the Scots. With the removal of the court the nobility lacked a political focus, the burgesses detected a detrimental effect on Scottish trade. In controlling the privy council and the Lords of the Articles James had drawn the teeth of parliament; Charles seemed bent on silencing it forever. His Act of Revocation of 1625 attempted to solve the three-fold problem of crown finance, ecclesiastical endowment and the collection of church revenues by compelling the surrender of church lands in lay hands. Although unsuccessful this act, coupled with a proposal to abolish heritable jurisdictions, both panicked and antagonised the nobility and landowners. Arbitrary and increased taxation lent fuel to the flame.

An identification in the minds of some Scots of church and nation rendered the Kirk the powder keg of the impending holocaust. Many laymen involved themselves in church courts (such as kirk sessions) as a means of alleviating political frustration. In the Lowlands a steady erosion of the kin-ties created a proportional reliance upon the paternalism of the church. Charles' obsession with liturgical revision, of foreign inspiration and smacking of popery, was anathema to the Scots. His tendency to advance churchmen (including bishops) in civil affairs, culminating in the appointment of Archbishop Spottiswoode as chancellor in 1635, caused great alarm. Many held the assertion of parliamentary sovereignty to be the obvious counter-weight to royal prerogative but parliament was muzzled and supplication rejected. Charles' arbitrary imposition of a new code of canons in 1636 reinforced such a view.

The Scots considered that much was innovatory, popish and heretical in the prayer book of 1637, described by Montrose as 'the brood of the bowels of the whore of Babel'. Its public reading in St Giles was the signal for revolt. Edinburgh swarmed with petitioners demanding its withdrawal; rioting and mobbing were daily occurences. Montrose was elected as a representative of the nobility to a committee of petitioners known as the 'Tables', which provided a forum for opposition and functioned as a substitute parliament. As a privy councillor it was Argyll's duty to attempt to control the situation. Not for a year did he align himself with Montrose.

In February 1638 Alexander Henderson, minister of Leuchars, and the lawyer, Johnston of Wariston drew up the National Covenant. One of the first to subscribe it was Montrose, so infected by the excitement of the times, that he was prophetically told he would never be at rest until 'lifted up above the rest in three fathoms of rope'. Such delirium was widespread. The kirks

20 A rosary and crucifix used by Mary

19 Mary, Queen of Scots

21 Lord Darnley

22 Lochleven Castle, Kinross-shire

23 John Knox

24 Hermitage Castle, Roxburghshire

25 James VI as a child

26 George Buchanan

27 Linlithgow Palace, West Lothian

28 Crichton Castle, Midlothian

29 Earl Patrick's Palace, Kirkwall, Orkney

30 The first Marquis of Montrose

31 The first Marquis of Argyll

32 Execution of Charles I

33 The Battle of Dunbar (from a contemporary plan)

34 Sir William Bruce's Kinross House, Kinross-shire

35 The first Duke of Lauderdale

36 Crathes Castle, Kincardineshire

37 Late 17th century silverware

38 Slezer's prospect of Perth, 1693

39 The Riding of Parliament, 1685

were packed, pews occupied for hours on end; the intellectual fodder of the revolution was provided by the pulpit and thousands came to feed.

The Covenant exploited the widespread fear of popery and the advance of Antichrist. It listed all statutes in favour of the reformed religion, so conferring a novel status on Scottish parliamentary legislation and signifying the constitutional struggle to come. Just as 'banding' was the traditional means of ensuring protection and maintenance, the Covenant was conceived as a bond for the maintenance of religion. It also owed a great deal to the concept of federal theology which preoccupied a number of the followers of Andrew Melville. There was also an Apocalyptic element. The Scots shared the widely-held seventeenth century belief that the Second Coming as prophesied in the Book of Revelation was imminent. In the minds of some, Scotland's divine and historic role was to prepare the world for this event. The need for preparation, however, precluded a total obsession with other worldliness. The legislation of the Covenanters is pervaded with a desire to reform society as a whole. Not only private morality but the improvement of industry, trade, agriculture, as well as poor relief and educational reforms are encompassed within their vision. The commitment in the Covenant to defend both religion and king would cause the rift between Argyll and Montrose. The former did not consider the interests of church and king to be always compatible; Montrose did. In 1638 the main strength of the Covenant was that it was all things to all men. It was both the focus of Scottish nationhood and the symbol of revolution. Those who took up arms to defend it appealed to patriotism and the fear that Stewart despotism would reduce Scotland to the status of a province.

Royal sanction was obtained for the first meeting of a general assembly for twenty years. When Hamilton attempted to dissolve the Glasgow assembly of November 1638 on the grounds that it was unconstitutional, Argyll spoke against him. According to Wariston, his declaration for the Covenant at this point 'incouraged and strengthened the cause mor nor if he had doone it befor'. The thwarted Hamilton distinguished Argyll as 'the dangerousest man in the state'. The assembly proceeded with the annulment of canons and liturgy and the deposition of the bishops. To his dying day Montrose would reject the bishops. With Argyll he played a leading role in suppressing internal opposition to the

Covenant and in achieving the capitulation of the king. Their disagreement arose over a subsequent course of action.

The problem of the legality of resistance had taxed the ingenuity of commentators for centuries. Medieval theorists believed that kingship was divinely sanctioned but that God might engineer the removal of the tyrannical monarch. Montrose was at one with John of Salisbury, who first formulated resistance theory in the twelfth century, in asserting that 'patience in the subject is the best remedy against the effect of a Prince's power too far extended'. The means of obtaining moderate government was 'to endeavour the security of religion and just liberty', both safeguarded by law and parliament. 'And if Parliaments be frequent and rightly constituted, what favourite counselour or statesman dare misinforme or mislead the king?' The essentially medieval notion that the king must be rescued from bad counsel justified the subscription of the Covenant. Having secured the religious demands and regular parliaments, Montrose feared the further diminution of royal prerogative. The tyranny of subjects was 'the most fierce, insatiable and insupportable tyranny in the world'.

Argyll also basically believed in a balanced constitution but he held that 'nothing is impossible or unfeasible for an enslaved people to do against tyrants'. He was more keenly aware of the split between king and kirk presaged by Andrew Melville's 'Two Kingdoms' theory. The presbyterian concept of parity in religion could easily be extended to the secular sphere. 'Popular furies would never have end, if not awed by their superiors', wrote Argyll, 'the people will soon learn their own strength and from thence infer that the popular power excels that of the noblesse'. He believed that the historical role of the Scottish nobility was to serve the king and defend the people, 'every one . . . his Majesty's shadow our care should ever be to carry ourselves to his people, as we desire his Majesty should appear to them and so make up to him a treasure of their love'. As one well grounded in the works of George Buchanan, who had refined resistance theory to justify the deposition of Mary, Queen of Scots, he could envisage the possibility of supplanting the king altogether. Such an awareness was no doubt heightened by his position as clan chief. He well knew that the 'misthryving' of the chief could result in his rejection, as he found to his cost in later years.

One of the most perceptive of contemporary historians, Gordon of Ruthven, remarks that the King of Scots 'is kinge of men . . . not intituled efter the countrie as other kingcs, but efter the natione', a useful fiction for king and subjects alike. Charles alienated the strong Scottish attachment to monarchy, which as Argyll observed, favoured the regulation of monarchy rather than its destruction. Montrose and Argyll disagreed as to the extent of such regulation.

Charles' visit to Scotland in 1641 was long remembered by the Scots as the year in which the sovereignty of parliament was asserted at the expense of royal prerogative. He was forced to ratify the legislation of the truly revolutionary session of 1640 which met in defiance of prorogation. A spate of legislation included compulsory subscription of the Covenant, the abolition of the Committee of Articles, and a Triennial act ensuring a parliament every three years. In 1641 he was further compelled to allow that henceforward virtually all civil appointments be made with the advice of parliament. He experienced 'tyranny of subjects' with a vengeance.

Montrose challenged the legality of the 1640 parliament. Neither the sinister reply that 'to do the less was more lawful than to do the greater', nor suggestions that a dictatorship and a canton north of the Forth be established for a nameless, if obvious, candidate, assuaged his growing uneasiness. His 'Cumbernauld Bond' subscribed by eighteen similarly alarmed individuals expressed anxiety at 'the particular and indirect practicking of a few'. He countermanded Argyll's discovery of the bond with allegations that 'King Campbell' was plotting Charles' deposition. While Argyll may well have nurtured such ambitions, that he would have voiced them in any but the most general terms is inconceivable. He certainly could be imprisoned while the testimony of witnesses was examined. Most gave vague statements but the evidence of one John Stewart occasioned a stream of oaths from MacCalein Mor. 'Many wondered thereat', but he was acquitted of treasonable intent.

From prison Montrose begged an audience with the king to impart information of the greatest importance, but before this could be granted, Argyll fled Edinburgh due to a plot on his life. The 'Incident' is an obscure affair with some basis in reality. Some of Montrose's sympathisers discussed the kidnapping of Hamilton and Argyll; the intended victims just possibly publicised the plot to increase their political capital. They returned unscathed in greater favour than ever. Argyll was given a marquisate. Shortly thereafter Montrose, who was incapable of influencing Charles against his favoured subject, was released largely through Argyll's good offices. News of calamitous events elsewhere in his dominions necessitated Charles' departure from Scotland; the Catholics had risen in Ireland.

Montrose's worst fears were realised in the Scottish commitment to the Solemn League and Covenant of 1643. Military support for the English Parliamentarians constituted armed rebellion. He rightly believed that English Independents were cynically using the idea of an international presbyterian crusade for political ends. The ideal of a presbyterian establishment in England, Ireland and Scotland 'according to the example of the best reformed churches', a phrase narrowly interpreted by the blinkered Scots, would remain a pious aspiration. During the negotiations on the second Covenant Charles frantically attempted to win over Argyll who characteristically withheld support for either side until the last possible moment. He was finally swayed by the king's acceptance of a cessation of fighting in Ireland where the Roman Catholics, widely credited with large scale massacres of Protestants, were to retain such possessions as they had won.

Catholicism was what Argyll feared most. Irish Franciscans claimed several thousand converts in the Hebrides in the 1620s. In 1626 Iain Muideartach, chief of Clanranald informed the pope of his willingness to lead a crusade to restore Scotland to catholicism. Gaelic-speaking Scots and a majority of Irish chieftains, 'from whose stock first we sprang', would co-operate. Many of the clans mentioned had ancient scores to settle with the Campbells. Even before Argyll declared for the Covenant, Charles and Hamilton discussed the exploitation of this antipathy. In 1639 the king commissioned Donald Gorm of Sleat and the earl of Antrim, an Irish MacDonald, as his lieutenants in the Highlands. Shortly thereafter Donald along with MacLeods, MacLeans and Clanranald himself planned the logistics of a descent on Argyll territory. The charge that Argyll used the Covenant to further his own interest is therefore correct, but he had no choice. The anti-Campbell coalition, so important in the seventeenth and eighteenth centuries was the brainchild of Charles I. In explaining their attachment to the Stewart cause the conservatism of the clans was matched by a desire to recover territory held by the Campbells. Thus an army held itself in readiness, waiting for a leader; and in return for cessation the Irish Catholics promised Charles military assistance. Antrim finally sent some fifteen hundred men to Scotland under the command of the legendary Alasdair MacDonald, young Colkitto. The Catholic crusade was being waged on Argyll's own doorstep.

Argyll, recognising Montrose's military ability, twice tried to woo him to his cause. Montrose refused, went to Oxford where he convinced Charles of his loyalty, and on 1 February 1644 he was commissioned as Lieutenant-general in Scotland with a marquisate to follow. So began the Glorious Year and the greatest adventure of Montrose's life.

Disguised as a groom, he penetrated the Covenanting lines and joined up with Colkitto in Athol. The two men complemented one another beautifully. Montrose had the gift of inspiring his followers to achieve the impossible; characterised by the MacVurich shenachie as 'active, intellectual and courageous', he overcame the rivalries of the clans by sheer force of personality. Colkitto was a proven warrior, a tower of strength who understood the warfare of the hills. In his one surviving letter to Argyll, Montrose enjoined him to submit to Charles, 'ready to embrace his penitent children . . . although provoked with unspeakable injuries'. The alternative was reduction by force. 'I rest your friend if you please . . .' Friendship was impossible. Argyll replied by mustering an army to pursue the elusive Graham.

At Tibbermore (1 September 1644) the cry of 'Jesus and no quarter' did not avail the Covenanting army. Montrose scored his first dazzling victory. Hard pressed by Argyll he then marched north where he sacked Aberdeen. Then began one of the wild marches for which Montrose is famous, a frantic manoeuvering for position on the draught-board of the Highlands, through Strathavon, Tomintoul, Rothiemurchus, Abernethy, Badenoch, Deeside and Strathbogie. At Fyvie he was almost caught napping, believing Argyll to be far to the south, but Montrose eluded his incompetent adversary.

Montrose's dilemma was that he could frolic in the Highlands till Judgment Day so far as the Lowlanders were concerned. Whenever he crossed the Highland line the clans deserted. With winter advancing Colkitto advocated a descent on the lion's den. Montrose

Fig 4 The Montrose Campaigns

tended to agree with the Campbells that it was 'a far cry to Loch
Awe' and even farther in winter, but his doubts were overcome.
His army marched along Loch Tayside through Crianlarich to
Glen Orchy and the fabled Loch Awe. Argyll hastened to
Inveraray, confident of picking off the starving and frozen royalists
at leisure. Once home he learned the incredible. Montrose was
advancing down Glen Shirra. Loch Fyne offered an escape route.
He took it, leaving several hundred clansmen to die and the riches
of Argyll to the marauders. This enterprise 'did shaike the
grandour of MacCalein with such terrible and shivering fitts, as
that great oake did bow lyke a reid before the wind'.

Argyll realised his stock was low and, supplied with reinforcements, he insisted on personally pursuing the invader as befitted
the clan chief. Having retreated through Appin, Loch Levenside
and Mamore to the Great Glen Montrose looked to be trapped between Mackenzie of Seaforth ahead and Argyll behind. Ingenuity,
fortitude and desperation took him up the Tarff and down Glen
Roy in the harshest of winter conditions among the highest moun-
tains in Britain. At Inverlochy on 2 February, he took an in-
credulous Argyll completely by surprise. He had been robbed of
command by a fall from his horse and could only observe the
onslaught from afar. The bitter lament of a Campbell widow
condemned a chief who took to the loch and left his kindred to
their fate. A jubilant Montrose informed Charles that he would
soon 'have reduced this country to your Majesty's obedience and
conquered from Dan to Bersheeba'.

Further honours were gained at Auldearn and Alford and in
August 1645 he won another victory at Kilsyth, an anguished
Argyll escaping by water for a third time. Intoxicated royalists
like the poet Drummond of Hawthornden considered 'the Golden
Age is returned ... the many-headed monster near quelled'. To
others the Graham's achievements were 'above what can be attributed to mankind'. Scotland appeared to belong to Montrose.

Yet the optimism was premature. At his triumphal entry to
Glasgow his Highlanders were already melting away like the
proverbial snow off a dyke. Colkitto departed to let more
Campbell blood. He transformed his ancestral Kintyre into a
smoking ruin and even after the Covenanting army had butchered
his clansmen at Dunaverty in 1647 Argyll was still directing
relief operations. Colkitto met a violent death in Ireland some

months later. Montrose's military success owed much to Colkitto and the Highland terrain; he was ill-suited to Lowland warfare. In attempting to break through to England and the king he was surprised by David Leslie and his experienced cavalry. At Philiphaugh (13 September 1645) the Glorious Year ended in a bloodbath. Montrose would have chosen death on the battlefield but, persuaded to flee, he returned north to spend an abortive year attempting to reorganise resistance. Meanwhile Charles had surrendered to the Scottish army; he commanded Montrose to disband his troops. September 1646 found the marquis aboard a sloop bound for continental exile.

Although Argyll continued to correspond with Charles he no longer believed that any agreement was possible. He rejected the Engagement, an undertaking made by Hamilton to assist the king in return for a presbyterian establishment, on the lines favoured by Montrose. On the defeat of the Engagers at Preston in 1648 he immediately contacted Oliver Cromwell who visited Edinburgh. Cromwell was much impressed by Argyll's political dexterity in purging parliament of the Engager majority but in spite of their mutual respect the brief alliance was an unnatural one.

Against his better judgment Argyll was forced to rely increasingly on 'the airie opinion of the clergie'. On his later admission he was beginning to lose his grip: 'my thoughts became distracted and myself encountered so many difficulties in the way, that all remedies applied had the quite contrary operation'. The parliament of 1649 set about the creation of the new Zion during Scotland's brief and unhappy experiment in theocracy. Royalists were excluded from office; lay patronage was abolished; death was decreed for blasphemy, idolatry, parent cursing, incest and witchcraft; the codification of Scots law was discussed. But Argyll was disgusted by the outrageous demands of the ministers. He attempted to exploit widespread revulsion at the execution of Charles on 30 January 1649 by reaching some accommodation with his heir.

The exiled Montrose was the darling of Europe. If he fretted at the inactivity of the court in exile, the king's execution gave him a fatalistic firmness of purpose. For two days he retired from the world to emerge encased in black armour, determined to sing Charles' 'obsequies with trumpet sounds' and write his 'epitaph in blood and wounds'. Argyll's envoys arrived at the Hague to trade Charles II a throne for his signature of the covenants. Although Montrose still adhered to the 1638 covenant he realised Charles was no Covenanter and his innate honesty compelled him to advise against signing; he would attempt restoration by conquest. The young king, however, continued to negotiate with the Scots even as he sent Montrose to his death. A tragic charade was beginning; Montrose would die for a deceitful king; Argyll would welcome a covenanted king he knew to be insincere; Charles II would sign anything for a hollow title.

The marquis's last campaign was quickly over. Landing in Orkney he added some thousand Orcadians to half as many Danish and German mercenaries. They crossed the Pentland Firth to be cut to pieces by the army of the Estates at Carbisdale on the River Oykell on 25 April 1650. Montrose, again persuaded against a warrior's death, spent two days in the wilderness of Sutherland only to be captured by MacLeod of Assynt and surrendered to the victors.

Since he had already been condemned as a traitor in 1644, no trial was required after the long ride to Scotland's Jerusalem. He was met in the Canongate by the local justice officers and, bound to a seat in the hangman's cart, the procession trundled uphill to the Tolbooth. Argyll once observed that 'whatever honour we have at the crime, we immediately forget and pity the criminal when he comes to suffer'. So with James Graham. The Edinburgh mob primed to stone the traitor, was reduced to tears at his passing. As the cart passed Moray House the eyes of Montrose and Argyll met briefly before the latter 'creipit in at the windows'. If Argyll read his own destiny in that gaze it is not recorded. At that very moment a letter from Charles was en route to Edinburgh disowning Montrose. When his own time came he could expect cold comfort from the 'merrie monarch'.

In prison Montrose penned his farewell to the world:

> Let them bestow on ev'ry Airth a Limb;
> Open all my Veins, that I may swim
> To Thee my Saviour, in that Crimson Lake;
> Then place my pur-boiled Head upon a Stake;
> Scatter my Ashes, throw them in the Air:
> Lord (since Thou know'st where all these Atoms are)
> I'm hopeful, once Thou'lt recollect my Dust,
> And confident Thou'lt raise me with the Just.

I

On 21 May 1650 he walked down the High Street to the Mercat Cross and a thirty foot gallows, dressed in all his finery 'more like a bridegroom than a criminal'. On the scaffold he made a short speech denying he had sinned against man and owning his king and his God. He paid the executioner, ascended the ladder, cried God's mercy 'on this afflicted land' and was pushed off. Argyll had been up all night while his wife gave birth to a daughter 'whois birthday', he wrote, 'is remarkable in the tragick end of James Grahame... He got sum resolution... how to go out of this world but nothing at all how to enter into ane other'. His sober report is remarkable not so much for its lack of charity as its total absence of vindictiveness towards a man who had consistently opposed him for the past ten years and who had totally destroyed his credit as a military leader. He was to learn that life can be more vexatious than death and in the following years he must sometimes have envied Montrose his fate.

Two months later Charles was in Scotland playing the role of the covenanted king in a bitter farce. His experiences in his ancestral kingdom fostered a lifelong detestation of the covenants, presbyterianism and Scotsmen. He was not only lectured incessantly by worthy divines but was also forced to renounce his parents. King Campbell was dead but Argyll the king-maker effectively rendered Charles impotent. He gambled on the Scottish affection for monarchy and his own control of the king to counteract widening divisions in the Covenanting ranks. His plans were foiled when Cromwell defeated the Scots in 'the brunt or essential agony of the battle of Dunbar'. David Leslie had effectively outgeneraled Cromwell who was retreating to England, but the ministers and the Estates attempted to transform Leslie's troops into a 'Gideon's Army' by purging undesirable elements. When the depleted Scots advanced down the rain-soaked slopes of the Lammermuirs near Dunbar on 3 September the strong right arm of the Lord was shattered and Scotland went to pieces. The Whigamores of the south-west attributed defeat to Charles' insincerity. Some joined 'God-intoxicated' Oliver who occupied the south of Scotland; others fought him. Within six months of Montrose's execution his supporters were the uneasy allies of MacCalein, grouped around the king. In a final throw of the dice Argyll himself set the crown on the king's head. A marriage between Charles and a Campbell was briefly considered and rejected. Argyll now went down the wind. He dismissed Charles' proposed invasion of England as folly and retired to Inveraray. Defeat at Worcester proved him right and placed Scotland at Cromwell's feet.

Totally devoid of political strength his attempts to manoeuvre for position were universally condemned as 'juglings and dissembling devices'. The Cromwellians considered him to be 'the last person any way considerable that standeth out', but in August 1652, threatened with an invasion of Argyll he undertook to live peaceably under the English government though he continued to pray for his 'distress'd prince'.

Montrose had jestingly warned that his ghost would haunt Scotland and Montrose Redivivus did stalk the Highlands. In 1653 the earl of Glencairn led an abortive rising. Argyll's son, Lorne, supported the royalists. He was a complex man whose idea of fun was 'a hundred good stories over a four hour drink' and who, in true Campbell fashion, was constantly at loggerheads with his father. While their unhappy relationship was well publicised, the recalcitrant offspring was a useful device which almost saved Argyll at the Restoration. The Campbells simply resorted to the age-old ploy for the preservation of estates, placing father on one side, son on the other. Lorne's intercession for his father's life in 1661 was unsuccessful but the estates did remain intact.

The commander-in-chief of the English administration was George Monk, the first man to succeed in containing the Highlands, partly by the intelligent establishment of garrisons at Inverness, Inverlochy and Perth, partly through enlightened and conciliatory policies. He it was who in the end engineered the restoration of Charles II and who betrayed his sometime ally, Argyll. One of Argyll's last public acts was his opposition to the Act of Union of 1657, on the grounds that it neither safeguarded religion nor Scots law, nor was taxation proportional to that of England. The man who had once envisaged 'all of one language, in one island, all under one king, one in religion, yea one in Covenant', demanded a union on equal terms or not at all.

In 1660 Argyll hastened south to greet Charles, was refused an audience and shipped back to Scotland to stand trial for treason. While he was imprisoned in Edinburgh castle the flag was flown at half mast, not on behalf of its illustrious captive, but to mark the burial with full honours of the reassembled remains of the Marquis of Montrose. He occupied his time compiling a little volume *Instructions to a son*, which shows he was in no doubt of the outcome of his trial. 'Infinitely unhappy are they who survive their credit and reputation', he wrote, 'There is no better defence against the injuries of fortune and vexation of life than death'. Much of the case centred on a topic dear to Argyll's heart – how answerable was a man for actions performed in his public capacity as a member of government? The able defence of George Mackenzie (the 'Bluidy Advocate' of Covenanting mythology) suggested minimal personal responsibility. To his intense relief and delight he was acquitted of any part in the execution of Charles I. The prosecution made little headway until Monk furnished the court with correspondence proving the defendant's complicity with the Cromwellians, which was, as Argyll said, 'the epidemical fault of the whole nation'. On the scaffold he counselled his audience to adhere to God and the covenants in the 'sinning and suffering time to come'. Then (27 May 1661) the guillotine known as the 'Maiden' devoured her victim. His head was placed on a spike on the Edinburgh Tolbooth, recently vacated by that of Montrose.

The beliefs of an age are often the key, as they are frequently a barrier, to the understanding of it. Both Montrose and Argyll died convinced of their own righteousness. If the former saw himself as an Old Testament general fighting for a Davidic king, Argyll could remark, 'We are not born for ourselves ... Moses the man of God chose rather to suffer affliction with the people of God than to enjoy the pleasures of sin for a season'. They chose different roads to salvation albeit one such route was straighter than the other. In the final analysis both subscribed to the sentiment of Montrose's famous verse :

> He either fears his Fate too much,
> Or his Deserts are small,
> That puts it not unto the Touch,
> To win or lose it all.

If both lost in the short term, the verdict of history places both among the victors, in the annals of Scotland the nation.

CHAPTER IX

Restoration and Revolution

Rosalind Mitchison

The central fact of this period is that both restoration and revolution were made in England. They were not decisions made by Scots nor were they made with a view to Scottish needs or wishes. If they were acquiesced in by most of the 'political nation' in Scotland this was because of a recognition of superior English military and economic strength, and in each event a significant section of Scottish society did not acquiesce. The opposition elements thus gave rise to two movements, the Covenanters, predominantly of the south-west, in the restoration period and the Jacobites, predominantly of the north, after 1689. Both these movements have received one-sided historiographical treatment: the earlier movement has been regarded as religious and the later as political. We will understand both better if we accept that the religious and political impulses of the two were in related proportions. They were both movements against the established political structure and its ecclesiastical policy. In the convenanting movement politics seem to be the foundation impulse: the Covenanters would not accept as godly any government not chosen by themselves, and were prepared to wage war on the ungodly. In the Jacobite movement the two motives were more evenly mixed. Jacobitism drew from a confused mixture of loyalism, catholicism, distaste for any but episcopal government and hatred of the house of Argyll.

English dominance was, at least in 1660, masked by the fact that England could not in practise run Scotland. With the disappearance of the military dictatorship of the Protectorate went the capacity to do so, in troops, in money and in the political stability necessary for a sustained policy of interference. Scotland therefore had to work out her solution within the framework of the general political settlement. This structure imposed a certain element of political stability on the country, but left open a wide area for development. The response to this was, on the whole, remarkable in achievement; it was shown in politics, law, the arts and intellectual life, and even in the temporary middle way of a working relationship between episcopal and presbyterian church government. In some aspects the current of activity was shared with England, and may even have been derived from there, but on the whole it is still true to look on Scottish culture in this period as self-sustained, when Scottish government was not.

The restoration did not simply mean the return of Charles II, but also of his machinery of government: the privy council and parliament, the social sector that controlled these (the nobility) the courts, and a church at least nominally episcopal. For none of these elements was restoration a simple return to the past. Once the restored parliament had got into its stride it passed the Act Rescissory, annulling all legislation since 1633, but in fact the clock could not be put back so simply. Crown, nobility and church had all changed during the interregnum. It took everyone some time to appreciate the depth of this change.

The prospect for Scottish development did not look particularly bright in the early 1660s. 'Restoration' always includes a *revanche* element, anxious to pay off old scores. As always after revolution and war there was little to pay them with. To the poverty of Scotland from economic backwardness had been added the poverty from over-taxation and English occupation and the further depression of economic life by a decade of government in English economic interests. If England after 1660 no longer directly regulated Scotland's trade, English jealousy and rivalry circumscribed it. There were direct English restrictions on the import of Scottish commodities, coal and salt, both valuable exports. More seriously there were indirect influences from the continuing rivalry between England and the Netherlands for trade supremacy and the wars into which this dragged the British crown.

The future looked bad also because of the hold of the Covenant (by which was now meant the Solemn League and Covenant) over men's minds. Fanaticism was not easily got out of the system in spite of the political failure and religious division that it had caused. 'Covenant theology' had orignally evolved as a method of preaching morality within the framework of predestination, but with the national covenants this had given way to a concept of a binding legal settlement, dictating political and religious policy and impervious to political facts. The insistence of the 'remonstrant' minority that it was the true Kirk had torn in two both church and state. The split had been perpetuated for government ends under the protectorate and now gave rise to unrest in lowland Scotland, particularly in Galloway and in Fife. The south-western section of this movement was the first significant political activity in Scotland which did not rely on leadership from the nobility, and its existence is a powerful reminder of the change produced in the position of the nobility by their enforced submission, first to the Kirk and secondly to the English in the 1650s. The nobility could not be fully restored in authority, and in the government's brusque attempt to do what it could in the direction of such restoration lay the origin of the large body of unbeneficed presbyterian clergy. The restoration of patronage, and the explicit acknowledgement of episcopacy that accompanied it, forced out over two hundred and fifty ministers in 1662, and these formed a nucleaus of propaganda and resistance throughout this period. The schism was kept alive by the strong professional identity of the clergy. Society did not yet accept the idea of re-ligious or social dissent, so a movement of this kind could not hope to be passive. It was, in fact, a continual source of violence in a country which could not afford, and did not know how to ad-minister, any system of regular policing.

So in the 1660s both poverty and division cast a gloom over the outlook. There were, however, some gains from the last thirty years which gave ground for optimism. To begin with there had been a distinct, if hesitant, step in the direction of the secularisation of politics and society everywhere outside the em-battled areas of covenanting strength. The king himself had cut down the share of eccelesiastics in government, and was determined that neither they nor religious motives should openly dictate policy. Episcopacy was restored because it was convenient as an instru-ment for governing the church and for controlling parliament and because it helped to keep the two kingdoms together, but it was not emphasized or given any sacramental function. Ministers ordained by presbyters were not required to seek reordination. Though the Kirk still controlled a great part of life, religion and the rival claims of church and state to authority had a less total hold on men's minds. The awakening intellectual interests of the country are evidence of this.

Another sign of improvement is that from 1660 to 1690 the food supply and population of the country seem to have achieved a better balance than had been there before. Though the years

1659–60 appear to have been ones of food shortage and the harvest of 1674 fell badly short of need, the period as a whole was one of adequate supply. Whether this was the result of a larger area under cultivation and better transport, or whether it was also the result of a population reduced by emigration and death in earlier decades, we cannot say at present, and probably never shall be able to say. All we can say is that for most of this period most areas of the country produced enough food to feed their inhabitants, and at times there was even some for export.

A further advantage was that by the 1660s in much of lowland Scotland schooling had come into existence. The Act of 1633 requiring parishes to provide a school and schoolmaster had been widely implemented. General education, demanded by the *First Book of Discipline,* had been made a nationally accepted aim, and was well on the way to be an established fact. The response made by the East Lothian parish of Yester to the rigours of invasion, battle, plunder and conquest in 1650–1 was a small scale image of this. As soon as life had become sufficiently normal after the battle of Dunbar for the kirk session to meet again, it applied all available funds to the schooling of poor children. By 1660 the bulk of lowland parishes had a school, and had had it long enough to have a good supply of literate adults, a fact which had considerable influence on the problem of government in both church and state. A literate public was familiar with the doctrine of Calvin and could be schooled by the catechism. It was familiar with biblical imagery and biblical passions. Sermons were expositions of doctrine to a populace well trained in argument. In some ways this made the country more governable. Arguments of law and logic could be understood and used. The kirk session provided a local court in which men of no great social standing could exercise responsibility in business and government. But literacy also laid the country open to the propaganda of militant dissent. Much of the rhetoric of this section has all the crudities and distortions of the self-educated orator. Intemperate literature, polemical sermons, the use of the Bible as a textual lottery, all brought irrational and unforeseeable risks of rebellion.

Education was an achievement of the Kirk. It was the ministers who had pressed for it, and who persuaded the landowners to support it. Landowners and peasantry paid for the schooling of the children, but it was the Kirk which controlled and inspected it. This victory was a sign of the long established professionalism of the ministry, a body with its own discipline, way of life and sense of responsibility. The ministry had become a partly hereditary group. Sons of ministers went into the same profession : daughters married into it. It had spiritual as well as executive prestige. The profession had also personal links with the lesser landowning families, and the unified structure of Scottish education was beginning to bring forward a small peasant entry to the profession. The existence of this separate, self-conscious class of ministers was to provide one of the challenges of the period. How far was the restored government going to be able to incorporate them in its structure and hold their allegiance?

This professional class should be regarded as including all those in orders. The main mistake of the restoration was the decision to force out over a quarter of these men over the issue of patronage. There was no lack of alternative recruits : the Kirk could still be supplied with qualified ministers. But these would work under difficulties while the 'outed' ministers, even if of moderate opinions, remained at hand, to act as a focus for opposition in the parishes. And it was characteristic of the time that very few 'outed' ministers were moderates. They were men who had come to office during the accomplishment of the revolution in the period of ecclesiastical domination, when pulpits were the mouthpieces of political programmes. They had shared the conviction that God had placed the guidance of Scotland in the hands of their order; through them he had intended great things for the world. The language of the Old Testament, in which so much religious and political argument had been conducted, was not such as to advance the ideas of moderation if they had been acceptable on other grounds. The 'outed' formed a nucleus of opposition, for most of the time with physical impunity, and in many cases they made a network of an illegal alternative church. This church could be conducted by secret meetings, but when if felt strong enough preferred 'field preaching' which meant massive meetings in the open, at which attenders, as was usual in the seventeenth century, were armed. These meetings were dangerous in themselves, and still more dangerous in their effect on those outwith their body. Extremist organisations possessed of uncompromising argument have often exercised an attraction over the public in general when that public has been prepared to admit part only of the claims of the arguments. We have had numerous opportunities of appreciating this kind of influence in the twentieth century in which the base of the argument has been the overriding claims of nationalism rather than those of God. The pull of the Irish Republican Army on sentiment in Ireland, and of illegal Zionist organisations in the 1930s and 1940s in Palestine, are instances of the power of one over-simplified line of thought and propaganda on a public not prepared to disagree totally with the fundamental premise. In states lacking a well organised system of legal opposition, all the grievances of sections of the community (and clumsy governments inevitably provide such grievances) add to the pull of sympathy for the outlawed organisation. Seventeenth century Britain had yet to learn to accept the idea that there might be something wholesome in organised opposition. Neither the supporters nor the opponents of government yet allowed for the rights of the other. In Scottish politics (in particular) there was almost no mechanism in the 1660s for expression of patriotic dissent in politics. There was some mechanism in ecclesiastical matters because of the real attempt of this period to weld together the strengths of the presbyterian system with the political convenience of episcopacy.

It would be over-complimentary to see the new structure of bishops in presbytery as an attempt to get the best of both systems of church government. It seems rather to have been an inevitable compromise. There were again bishops ruling a church in which the presbyterian church courts were well established and with a large amount of presbyterian opinion. Since the split between remonstrant and resolutioner clergy made it impossible to hold a general assembly that both would accept, the highest court of the presbyterian system had to be dispensed with. But for short periods the vigour of a presbyterian system can spring from the parish and presbytery level, and these functioned as before. Only at the synodal level, not an important one in either presbyterian theory or practise, was it necessary for the two systems of church order to interact. The church structure was thus not so much a compromise as a partition. Compromise, however, spread over the area least suitable for it, the actual conduct of church services, in which minor liturgical vestiges were submerged in apparently spontaneous exhortatory prayer and vast sermons. The contemporary habit of referring to church services as 'sermons' shows how small the element of worship had become. All this 'compromise' was simply hand-to-mouth expediency. It was certainly better than religious persecution, but it left frustrated those who wanted an orderly liturgy and seemly services as well as those who thought the existence of bishops and lay patronage sinful. It was based on the principle of letting sleeping dogs lie. But, as British governments have discovered in this century, sleeping dogs have a way of waking up. Presbyterian sympathies survived, and with constant agitation from outside the church and occasional misgovernment within it, lost nothing in strength, while episcopal sentiment had little to hold to except the support of government.

Probably more influential for good in this period than the uneasy church settlement was the fact that the nobility had been tamed. No longer would they be able to 'band' and put pressure on the government. Tolerance of private feuding and organised violence, at least in the lowlands, was no longer necessary to government. Disputes had more and more to be settled by law, and this meant that the law had to develop, in content, in authority and in the professionalism of those who served it. Paradoxically not all the developments in the use of courts to settle disputes can be regarded as in the interests of stability and peace. In particular the way in which the earl of Argyll used his own court to build up an empire in the west over lands peopled by other clans, by Macleans, Stewarts, Camerons and Macdonalds, left a problem in political resentment on which most of Highland Jacobitism in the eighteenth century was to be based. But in general the use of courts, particularly those of the Crown, was an improvement on the use or threat of force. By removing the shadow of violence from overmighty neighbours it made possible the independence of lesser landowners, and so eventually, the unification of nobles and lairds in a landed interest and its contribution to the economic achievement and the culture, visual and verbal, of the eighteenth century.

Even in this period the signs of this development begin. The craggy, cramped towerhouses of the early seventeenth century are superseded by the classical adaptations of Sir William Bruce. Landed society, or at least a part of it, was prepared to appreciate good silver, elegant gardens, local history and science. It was beginning to turn to the idea of economic development, but there were sharp limitations in the concepts that it was as yet able to handle in this field. Wealth, it was dimly felt, might, and ought to, accrue mysteriously from some outside agency, from colonial trade or from a new industry brought in like an exotic plant from elsewhere. The need to integrate any new development to society and to the economy as a whole was not seen, nor was the basic need of improved management within the existing sectors. We have a picture of the limitations of the vision of the landed class in the *Glamis Book of Record,* where we see the young earl of Kinghorn restore the houses and estate of the family from the effects of his father's political mistakes. It is all done by care and rearrangement. If debts cannot be paid off then at least they can be placed in the hands of friends. At no point does the idea of increasing revenue by better economic exploitation came into the earl's mind. The political and economic disasters of his father had taught him to cut his coat according to his cloth but not to question whether the size of cloth was immutably fixed.

Improvement, at least of agriculture, lay far in the future. Meanwhile there were tastes and interests to be encouraged that would not only be one of the main springs of improvement but would further limit the share of life engulfed by religion. There was a long overdue relaxation in the limits of markets and the control of trade by established burghs, marked in particular by the Act of 1672 which made a severe dent in burghal privilege. This was a response of government to the demands of new or expanding activities, and indicates that economic interests were increasingly being regarded as a proper sphere of politics. There were more things for men to think about than the relations of church and state, and the 1680s appear to have been a period of relative, if limited prosperity. The Scottish privy council made a real effort to establish minor industries. The aim was to manufacture in Scotland the consumer needs of the upper classes : glass, paper, good quality woollen cloth for instance. None of these were notable successes but recent research has shown that some industries survived more hardily than we used to think. Appropriately enough one of the more enduring of these, paper, owed its existence not only to the indirect influence of increasing law and order but to the direct needs of the instruments of this progress, the lawyers' production of *paperasserie.*

Still, the developments of this period were very limited. Their significance stands as aims, not as achievements. The country moved away from famine and disorder, and slightly away from poverty and fanaticism. Progress was limited by the inadequacy of the instruments of government as well as by rigidities of mind and the influence of polemic. For much of the time one has the impression of a country at war. Immediately after the restoration there were still the effects of the heavy burden of taxation and occupation, and the need to pay for the demolition of the English fortresses. It soon became clear that the church settlement was to leave out a considerable minority who would attend conventicle but not church. These could not easily be persuaded or forced back into the fold, especially when there was a large body of clergy outside it. In some south-western presbyteries the entire body of ministers was 'outed'. Their charges were obviously unattractive since they subjected the occupiers to the risk of verbal and physical violence, so the occupiers, though of suitable ecclesiastical and political flavour, were not men likely to succeed in wooing back the recalcitrant. In the south-west the gulf in political and religious opinion between the nobility, often catholic, and their tenantry meant that though nobles could oppress their tenants they could not lead them. In the mid 1660s came the Dutch War, with increased taxation, and the futile rebellion by conventiclers that led to the scrambling fight at Rullion Green. The government showed that it had weapons and techniques suitable to the task of holding down a hostile population: execution, imprisonment and occasionally torture, as well as fines and the quartering of troops. It was using them in a haphazard way, the result of amateurishness combined with a basic lack of conviction. At best such techniques can only limit a hostile body: they are unlikely to convert it.

Things improved after Rullion Green with the government of Lauderdale and his attempt to meet dissent halfway. Compromise with those 'outed' who would make any sort of terms was the order of the day. There was some success in this, but the hard core of covenanting resistance was untouched, and the compromise itself involved asserting state powers over the church which caused much misgiving. The Act of Supremacy, (1669) in which the assertion was made, was crudely worded, but indirectly it showed the big social change of the restoration period, the shift in the balance of power, both in politics and in social structure, away from the clergy. Lauderdale's rule, which carried on through the 1670s, stood for compromise and lay culture as well as for personal profit. In fact one of its problems was the increased coherence of lay groupings. One of these was landed society, both nobility and gentry, which in these years developed the capacity to oppose the policy of the crown in parliament. Another was the lawyers, who were in fact a section of landed society. This is the period of the first organisation and lucid exposition of Scots law, culminating in 1681 with Stair's *Institutes*. The 1670s also saw the drawing together of the Faculty of Advocates into a professional group with their own loyalty and ethos. Pressures were building up for the adaptation of monarchical government to a system with a more active role for debate and opposition.

The 1680s would probably have been a difficult time for an old-fashioned type of government in Scotland, even if the covenanting issue had been solved. But it was far from solution. The illegal conventicles became large scale armed gatherings. Lauderdale's effective rule ended in 1679 with the murder by covenanters of Archbishop Sharp, the main connecting link of government in church and state, and the disorderly rebellion in the west that was crushed at Bothwell Brig. Again English politics dominated Scottish, for the attempt at moderation and conciliation was abandoned in 1683 with the unravelling of the elaborate structure of plots against the king's person in both countries. The close connection between politics and religion in Scotland meant that investigation of treason was also repression of religious extremism. This repression bred still more intemperate resistance. Covenanting leaders declared war on those who accepted the existing government; the government responded by shooting out of hand those who would not renounce this policy. In fact neither side, in this so-called 'killing time', killed very many of its opponents, but it was a time of fear on all sides. Murders by Covenanters and executions by troops were both arbitrary uses of force and created general fear.

The noticeable feature of the 1680s is that both sides were gradually deserted by opinion. The overt display of state control over the church included a Test Act which could not be accepted by any who hoped for any change in the church, whether presbyterian or episcopal in sentiment. The internal divisions of the Covenanters and their resort to brutality in 1679 also shook off supporters. In the 1680s it became impossible for sincere supporters of a presbyterian order to approve of them. It would be unrealistic not to allow some element of success to the more active and intelligent repression carried out by Claverhouse in the south-west from 1682. By forcing apparent conformity at the risk of fines he moved the issue from martyrdom to inconvenience. But the main element in reducing support for the Covenanters came from the clear indications that their movement was more concerned with politics than with prayer. The famous series of documents voicing covenant policy, from the *Sanquhar Declaration* to the *Apologetical Declaration* show this.

The most interesting and revealing of these documents is the *Queensferry Paper*. It is a medley of Whiggery in Scottish terms, that is the claim of the saints to choose a godly ruler, and in English terms, where the talk is of civil rights and of the end of government as the maintenance of all men in their rights and liberties. The ideas soon to be developed and published by Locke go hand in hand with the law given by God to Israel. The foreign elements of Whiggery are soon abandoned, but even so the argument moves inexorably from religion to politics. The Covenanters are committed to overthrowing the 'kingdom of darkness' in favour of the 'kingdom of Christ', and it is clear that these kingdoms are conceived as in this world. So the existing monarchy, all monarchy, is denounced. The Covenanters, as the true Kirk, now set up their laws and government for Scotland.

This can be seen as the last manifestation of the movement for a second reformation in the 1630s and 1640s. Its conservatism can be seen in the statement that the Covenanters cannot be accused of separation 'for if there be a Separation, it must be where the Change is, and that is not in us'. But the policies of the 'good old days', to which it looked back, had already led to disaster and conquest. Among those who had had sympathy for the covenanting ideal the *Queensferry Paper* may have brought home the realisation that this ideal would involve a return to chaos in both church and state. For the threat to church order was as direct as that to the state. The paper denounced as 'carnal' any form of majority rule by the presbyterian system. Those who believed in the divine right of presbytery could no longer support the Covenanters.

At the same time the succession of James VII in 1685 put a strain on those who saw the monarchy as a support of the episcopal church. James was an open catholic, whose policy of leniency to his own church was accompanied by leniency also to those outside the episcopal church. This left the established church without its main support, the government and law. The pressure the king brought to bear on all aspects of government in support of this policy was a reminder that the crown had still a repertoire of weapons inherited from days when unlaw and disorder had had to be countered by drastic action if they were to be countered at all. The use of such weapons in an era of relative stability brought into Scottish politics the idea of imposing limitations on the powers of government. Scottish opposition was coming to assume some of the ideas of English Whiggery, and in so doing was to bring the two countries closer together.

So the 1680s see the country turning to more secular politics, and beginning to think that political problems must be answered in terms of law, powers and administration, rather than in those of covenants with God. The movement in this direction was half-hearted. The episcopal church was not prepared to repudiate the king, even though he was a catholic, and the episcopal church had the willing or grudging support of many, probably of the greater part of the country. The unease that the trend to secular politics produced may be the reason why the only overt sign against James's government, the Argyll rebellion, gained no support. The Scots were prepared to put up with James. But they were also prepared to accept the ready made revolution against him from England. They would do more than just accept, and would use the occasion to put through parliament a verbose but important attack on the weapons of the crown, the *Claim of Right* (1689). They went on to establish openly the reality of parliamentary opposition that had been growing as a practice since Lauderdale's day and to make it effective by destroying the old Committee of the Articles, the crown's mechanism for control of parliament. The revolutionary settlement was to be ruthlessly presbyterian, against the new King William's wishes, with over two thirds of the existing clergy 'outed' in their turn. Since the only clergy uncontaminated by submission to bishops was the remnant of those thrown out in 1662 it was logical that this self-appointed true Kirk should insist on the rectification of the point on which they had been forced out and have lay patronage abolished. As, in fact, the ecclesiastical part of the new settlement was far more intolerant than the secular, it is not surprising to find that the opposition to the whole settlement, Jacobitism, was founded at least as much in religion as in politics. Secularisation was still incomplete, but it had come some way.

The revolution also signifies the acceptance of a change in the topic of government. The economic prosperity of the country had become a preoccupation of government, and private economic advantage had become normal and accepted aims for the upper class. The rising professional group of lawyers, laymen, would soon rival in influence the established group of the clergy. The country stood on the brink of a period of active experiment in lay government by privy council and parliament in uneasy harness together. The state had attempted even to set bounds to the actions of the clergy. In particular it attempted to moderate the vengeful policy of the presbyterian ministers. It was unsuccessful in this. The clergy were not prepared to observe the bounds set by the state. Wisely the government turned a blind eye to this resistance, and continued to assert that it was the effective ruler. In the long run it would be.

Though the Scottish revolution followed the English it did not do so peacefully, and the actual fighting of the revolution epitomised the changed nature of Scottish politics. In the summer of 1689 took place the battle of Killiecrankie and the siege of Dunkeld. The Highland clans that fought for James VII against his nephew William did so for secular reasons, from resentment at the Campbell domination that the revolution settlement would make permanent. On hearing the news of the Jacobite victory at Killiecrankie the privy council prepared to retreat to England. It recognised that England now set the stage of Scotland's politics by being ready to attempt reconquest of Scotland with English aid from beyond the border. It was saved from this step by the defence of Dunkeld. Dunkeld, and therefore Scotland, was held for the revolution by a 'regiment' of Covenanters, later to be known as the Cameronians. This 'regiment' was in origin a band of men engaged in 'rabbling' the episcopal clergy, forcing them from their parishes after the Revolution by threat of force. The apotheosis of this band into a regiment looked for a time like official reliance on fanaticism : but in a short while it became apparent that the 'regimental' aura had superseded the religious. Its habit of praying with sentries posted was a reminder that it was formed to enlist religion in the defence of the state. Behind this shield of force the politicians of Scotland were to carry on the

K

process of secularisation and learn the arts of political adjustment and the acceptance of reality in the 1690s, until English dominance, already the key to the new political system, became so overt that it had to be openly faced in the issue of Union.

CHAPTER X

Union of the Parliaments

T. C. Smout

Scotland in the period from 1690 to 1707 was a land of troubles that ran wide and deep beyond the games of politicians and the posturings of kirkmen. In many ways the man in the street and the man in the fields had other things to think about than saving the shreds of national parliamentary independence.

In the first place the 1690s was a decade of agricultural depression and famine : it began with low grain prices, but the years 1695, 1696, 1698 and 1699 were all associated with extremely high prices and wide-spread crop failure, exacerbated at the end by a severe winter, and cattle murrain. By 1700 it was all over. Farmers then began to renew their complaints of gluts of food on the market and low prices because no one would take it. This oscillation between extreme scarcity and high price in bad years and superfluity and very low price in good years provided the worst possible kind of economic environment for agricultural change. English visitors who came to Scotland from their own more advanced farming scenes were depressed by the wild landscapes devoid of enclosure, the weedy crops and thin animals : but what was the point of change if in one year you could not raise anything to sell and in another year scarcely sell anything you raised? The first tracts on improving husbandry were written in this period before the Union, but there were few able to profit from reading them.

We shall never know how many Scots died of hunger and associated diseases – especially 'famine-fever', typhus, which everywhere stalked in the tracks of dearth. Many stories were handed on for generations afterwards; about men dropping dead with grass or raw flesh in their mouths; about sons vainly trying to carry their father's corpse to be buried and falling from hunger by the way; about respectable tenants forced to beg bread for their children from pitiless neighbours who themselves succumbed later to the wrath of God. In some of the villages of the north-east graves are said to have been made just above high-water for those who died of hunger after trying to stay alive on the shellfish beds :

certainly in Dalkeith the kirk session ordered a lime pit to be dug for the bodies of those vagrants from the Borders who were trying to reach Edinburgh on the chance of finding food and who perished within sight of their destination. Edinburgh herself, with rare generosity, opened a kind of refugee camp in the Greyfriars kirkyard and distributed poor relief to the hungry irrespective of their parishes of origin. It was more usual to do as Stirling did, to list the town's own poor and relieve their need while refusing succour to the incoming stranger. There seems little doubt that the towns experienced much less hardship and disruption from the famine than the countryside, possible because they had efficient markets and the ability to import corn: the parish registers of Dumfries, for instance, show scarcely a quiver of exceptional mortality through the later 90s, but places like Spott in East Lothian and Kingsbarns in Fife, small rural parishes in very fertile counties, evidently suffered badly.

We tend to be very shocked by it all, in retrospect: contemporaries were not unmoved, but they did not see it in quite our light. There had been famines before, perhaps worse than this, certainly in the first half of the century and in the late sixteenth century. They were tragic, but they were the will of God, visitations on a sinful people – you could regard them as punishment for not having instituted a properly Covenanted church and king, as the Cameronian dissenters in the south-west did; or you could regard them as just deserts for the national pastimes of levity, fornication and Sabbath-breaking, as the Church of Scotland did; or you could regard them as 'King William's Ill Years', retribution for expelling the anointed James VII, as the Jacobites did. And although the period 1695–1700 did cause a severe jolt to the rural economy, it could in no way be said to have ruined it: by the early 1700s the position was back to normal, vacant holdings being absorbed again into cultivation and the old inefficient ways of husbandry being resumed because there seemed to be no alternative. Men had managed before to get over such times: no doubt they would have to manage again. Everyone who lived off the land was poor – landlord, tenant, cottar, crofter – in comparison to their English equivalents: but they had no reason to expect to become any poorer.

In the towns, however, the period 1690–1707 saw in some respects a deepening economic crisis. Partly this was the effect of war against France, which was waged at King William's behest from 1688 to 1697, and began again in 1701 to last until after the Union. War brought French privateers into the Firth of Forth and the Firth of Clyde: the Jacobites who had captured the Bass in 1692 made it a base for their activities and almost severed the supply line of the corn trade from the north-east coast to Leith. Scotland had no navy and could do little to defend herself until she commissioned a couple of frigates at the very end of the period: the Royal Navy under English command did little except use war as a pretext for stopping Scottish ships in the Clyde from sailing to the English colonies in America in contravention of the Navigation Acts. All this was ruinous to merchants: the Convention of Royal Burghs spoke of the 'great and unsupportable loss' and said that if privateers were not controlled 'the tread of the royall borrowes will be entirily destroyed and all merchants discouraged'. It was special pleading, but at times such a verdict did not look far wrong.

Furthermore a war against France was a war with Scotland's best trading partner (apart probably from England herself), and it entailed the loss of the valuable import trade in wine, brandy and salt on which there were high profit margins to be earned: it also cut off the chance of exporting herring, salmon, coal, wool and cloth which in earlier years had earned substantial sums by sales in France. Nor, unhappily, was there much chance of compensating for such losses by expanding trade to other markets. England took Scottish cattle and linen and some coal and corn, but placed tariffs and marketing restrictions upon them which seemed to restrict the possibilities of growth. Holland was beginning to reduce her intake of Scottish woollen cloth and coals, apparently because they could not compete for cost and quality on the Dutch market with alternative supplies: the same was true of salt and cloth (though not of fish or wool) in the Baltic. Altogether there were most ominous signs of the contraction of external markets to the Scottish merchant, and it was clear that even the return of peace would not put everything automatically right in the cities: but what could restore prosperity was not at once easy to see.

Town and country alike were, in these years, affected by the restoration of the church to a presbyterian polity. Admittedly there was no question of a return to the extreme forms of general assembly control which had characterised the heady days of the 1640s, and in wide areas north of the Tay it proved impossible even to remove episcopalian ministers from their manses and their kirks before the Union. But the restored assembly showed much enthusiasm for puritan forms of control, being no whit less anxious than the church under the bishops to punish fornication by the kirk stool, even more sabbatarian, and earnest in calling for fasts of repentance to avert the wrath of God. The Kirk instituted an examination of the schools and universities to make them more Godly and more efficient. One effect of the new regime was the withdrawal of favour from those who had done much to illuminate the reign of Charles II and James VII – Sir Robert Sibbald the naturalist and topographer, Archibald Pitcairne the physician and Sir William Bruce the architect : though all continued to work during the 90s, and perhaps Bruce's finest masion – the core of the present Hopetoun House – was built between 1699 and 1702. The saddest symbol of the intellectual climate of these years was a Unitarian student at Edinburgh, Thomas Aikenhead, executed for the blasphemy of denying the divinity of Christ on the testimony of one witness, and with the collusion and approval of the Edinburgh ministers. He has surely an even better claim to be regarded as a religious martyr than the rebellious and fire-eating Convenanters who had perished at the scaffold in the Grassmarket under the previous rulers. Scotland did not in the late seventeenth century welcome free discussion. We do well to recognise the deeply authoritarian and closed traditions of her society : we are certainly not dealing with a democracy which believed in maximising the opportunities for freedom and individual choice.

After the Revolution of 1690 the country was ruled under its new constitution with a certain increase in ostensible independence. The head of the state was King William : no one of course tampered with the Union of the Crowns. His representative in Scotland was the Commissioner, personnally appointed, and assisted by a nominated privy council : but the Lords of the Articles, the old steering committee of parliament, had gone, and parliament now could claim a degree of independence from the crown which none of its predecessors had enjoyed. There is not very much sign that around 1690 it felt much need to cherish this independence. There was a great deal of talk at the time of the Revolution of merging with the parliament of England in a Union of the type that came later : the king wanted it, the representatives to the Scottish convention wanted it (according to one account they were unanimous in their wish); even Andrew Fletcher of Saltoun, later to be the leading opponent of such a settlement, said 'we can never come to any true settlement but by uniting with England in Parliaments and Trade'. The main reason why it did not come about then was that the English did not want it at all. What had they to gain by sharing power with the rascally Scot? Yet the Scottish representatives were never again so anxious for union, or so uncritical of the distant monarch from whom the power flowed.

Two incidents in the 1690s in particular shook confidence in the king – Glencoe and Darien. The Massacre of Glencoe in 1692 was a nasty outgrowth of the problem of pacifying the Highlands which had bedevilled the government since the rising under Dundee in 1689. The Master of Stair, who held state office as secretary, determined to make an example of those who were still in rebellion against the crown. MacIan, the head of the Macdonalds of Glencoe, made his submission to the government, but it was rejected on a technicality, and King William signed and countersigned orders 'to extirpate' the clan. They were in fact put to the sword by the treacherous attack of a detachment of soldiers whom the Macdonalds had been entertaining peacefully in the glen for a fortnight; and although many escaped the chief himself and some thirty-seven of his men perished. The incident had nothing to do with the ancient Campbell – Macdonald feud even though the soldiers happened to belong to Argyll's regiment. Indeed, had it been merely an incident between 'barbarous' clans no one would have minded very much; the scandal was that the secretary and the crown should have been in collusion to attack a peaceful and unarmed band of men who believed themselves to have received the royal pardon. The reputation of William never recovered from this blow.

The second incident, the events that led to the failure of the Scottish colony at Darien, were more complicated and prolonged. The idea of creating a national plantation and a monopoly company to run it must be seen in the contexts, on the one hand, of envy of the imperial power of England, Holland and France and, on the other, of the depression in Scotland's traditional foreign markets in Europe. The idea can be traced back to a discussion in privy council as early as 1681. In 1693 forty-eight merchants and others of commercial experience and standing signed a bond calling attention to the 'great advantages that may redound to this nation by promoting a trade to the coast of Africa, America and other foreign parts', and in 1695 the king agreed to an Act which the Scottish Parliament had promoted setting up a Company of Scotland with a monopoly of trade to distant continents and with the right to make colonies and raise capital.

The moving spirits at this stage were almost certainly a group of London Scots who hoped, with English merchants' backing, to burst open the monopoly of the English East India Company, currently under pressure in the capital itself; maybe they hoped under the Scottish flag to move into Far East trade and to supply England as semi-legalised interlopers, much as the Ostend and Scandinavian East India Companies did in the eighteenth century. Certainly they hoped to raise half the capital in the south. Unfortunately they hopelessly miscalculated the power of the established East India interest in the Westminster Parliament: news of the moves in Scotland led eventually to the proscription of the Company of Scotland in England – its directors were threatened with impeachment and the attempt to get subscriptions was declared illegal. Nor was this all: English consuls abroad, especially at Hamburg, were successfully able to dissuade foreigners from investing, and the king unequivocally came down on the side of London, dismissing Lord Tweeddale as his Commissioner for his inability to keep the Edinburgh Parliament under control. Not for half a century had there been such a division of interest and bitter conflict between the two kingdoms in the union, and it was self-evident in Scotland that the monarch had no real interest in the north except to keep it as the leashed running-dog of the wealthier southern kingdom, on which his power as a monarch able to rule in state and to wage war on France ultimately rested.

Nevertheless the Scots pressed on with their scheme for a Company, raising what money they could within Scotland by popular subscription, and considering schemes on which they could base its trade. It was here that they made their fatal error. Persuaded by the visionary dreams of William Paterson, a London Scot of undeniable imagination and personal magnetism, deluded also by Lionel Wafer, a pirate surgeon who claimed to corroborate by his practical experience of the area the hopes of Paterson, the directors opted for settling at Darien on the Isthmus of Panama from whence they hoped to establish a great trading emporium with an opening to the Caribbean on one side and ultimately to the Pacific on the other. Two expeditions were sent out, the first in 1698, the second in 1699: the resources behind them were inadequate, the provisioning of the ships was bad, the standard of command at sea and on land deplorable (with a few exceptions). The colony was overwhelmed in the end by incompetence, disease and Spanish hostility. Everything was exacerbated by William's orders that no English colony was to give succour to the Scots, understandable enough since they were trying to settle in territory over which the Spanish claimed sovereignty at a time when William was trying to keep Spain out of a military alliance against France. Failure was inevitable from the moment the Scots, lacking resources, set their hearts on the swamps of the Isthmus of Panama, but the king's hostility gave them an opportunity to blame outside causes. At least one of the later efforts of the Company of Scotland to redeem its fortune by individual voyages to Africa and the Far East was successful, but not on the scale necessary to salvage its losses.

When the ultimate failure of the Darien scheme became known in Scotland in 1700 the mood of the country turned extremely bitter, very Anglophobic and very much against the king: there was talk of calling a Convention of Estates at Perth to defy the government, and men recalled the atmosphere of 1641. Nevertheless the Union of Crowns survived because the Scots were divided so deeply between the Jacobites and the rest, between Presbyterian and Episcopalian, between one political faction of grandees in parliament and another. Obviously, though, no one at this moment in Scotland was going to express a preference for a closer union with England, even as an economic panacea. There was no sense at all in which, as is sometimes suggested, the Scots 'had' to go into a fuller union because after the failure at Darien they 'had' to have access to imperial markets. On the contrary they were preparing to settle down in 1701 and 1702 to what one contemporary observer called a 'kind of glade poverty'. Darien led not to union, but to national disillusion and stalemate.

It was the death of William III and the accession of Queen Anne without heirs in 1702 which created the opportunity for a new political initiative: for the Union of Crowns to continue it

L

would be necessary for both parliaments to agree on one person to whom the crown should pass after the death of Anne. In its prevailing mood it was unlikely any recently elected Scottish parliament would knuckle under and meekly follow an English lead : the queen, impressed by her predecessor's advice in his latter days to solve the Scottish problem by amalgamating the two parliaments, appointed Scottish and English commissioners to negotiate to this end – after desultory conversations, in which the English showed less interest even than the Scots, these were broken off. The queen then had no alternative but to call for new elections in Scotland and to meet the problem head on. The New Parliament, to be the last to meet in Edinburgh up to the present time, assembled in May 1703 : the queen appointed the duke of Queensberry as her commissioner and hoped for the best.

The consequences for the Crown were a complete disaster. It was not perhaps the case that the members of the New Parliament were soaked in 'nationalist fervour in revolt against English domination and selfishness', but they were certainly much less under the control of the commissioner and the Westminster government than the last parliaments of William III had been : the latter had given the Crown trouble, but in the end they knew which side their bread was buttered and for reasons of self-interest did not press their opposition too far. The New Parliament was divided into three main factions – a 'Court' party, normally obedient to the commissioner, with about one hundred adherents; a Jacobite or 'Cavalier' party of about seventy; and a 'nationalist' group, the 'Country' party, of about sixty. In addition there were about a score of members who were known as the 'Revolution men', supporting the principles of the 1690 settlement in favour of an Hanoverian successor and broadly supporting the 'Court' party but not of it. The composition of the government tried to integrate as many of these factions as possible, and it had Cavaliers among the officers of state to the chagrin of the 'Revolution men', but nothing could disguise the fact that the Court party had no automatic majority and that there was therefore always the possibility of toppling Queensberry or of altering the coalition by embarrassing him. This has to be borne in mind to understand what followed.

The parliament in the course of 1703 presented for the royal assent two bills which greatly alarmed the queen and England. One became in 1704 the Act of Security and Succession, which declared that Scotland would not follow England into the Hanoverian succession except on conditions securing the Crown, parliaments, religion, liberty and trade 'from English or any foreign influence'. The other became the Act anent Peace and War, which reserved to the Scottish parliament the right to make treaties, alliances, peace and war; hitherto Scottish foreign policy had been the monopoly of the Crown, and therefore by the early eighteenth century practically the monopoly of the English cabinet. The motives for the passage of these bills were complicated : some hoped by doing so to defeat Queensberry or exclude a rival faction from office : some were swayed by the oratory of Andrew Fletcher of Saltoun, the most persuasive nationalist in the Country party who was seeking to limit the power of the Crown and the English government and to enlarge thereby the power of the Scottish parliament. There is not much evidence, however, of a concerted plan to abandon the Union of Crowns – rather of an atmosphere of dissatisfaction about how the existing constitution was working and a wish to embarrass an unpopular and vulnerable Commissioner.

The English government, however, was in no mood to examine the subtleties of northern party politics. It was at this point in 1704 that England became convinced the Scots were out to challenge royal authority, and that English safety was threatened by the danger in Scottish secession. A runaway Scotland, they thought, would quickly turn Jacobite and make common cause with France; things would return to the old menacing situation of the late middle ages when England could never venture an army abroad without a risk of attack from over the Tweed. Consequently they bent all their energies to the task of bringing Scotland into an Incorporating Union. The very arrangement which they had so contemptuously avoided considering on many previous occasions, and as recently as 1690 and 1702, became now their first priority.

In pursuit of their aim the English used four weapons; veiled military threats, economic sanctions, bribery and negotiation. The sanctions were largely embodied in the Alien Act of March 1705 which stated that unless Scotland either appointed new Commissioners for a Union of Parliaments, or adopted the Hanoverian succession by Christmas, Scottish estates in England would be confiscated and (more seriously) Scottish exports of linen, cattle and coal to England, would be prohibited. Imports of wool from

England, already illegal in theory, would now be effectively stopped. It cut right at the heart of Scottish trade, for with Scotland's flagging fortunes in European commerce her exports of cattle and linen to England and her export of raw wool (much of it originating in England) to the Continent constituted the greater part of her ability to earn foreign exchange. The Act was later rescinded, but the other threats remained, and pretexts were evidently found for preventing the movement of Scottish cattle over the border until after the Union.

Bribery was an alternative means of bringing pressure to bear: its nature, extent and effectiveness are matters widely disputed among historians. As it was done secretly it is naturally hard to substantiate in detail, but it can be shown that the duke of Argyll (who became commissioner in 1705 in succession to the marquis of Tweeddale, who had in turn succeeded the duke of Queensberry when he fell in 1704) was bribed by the promise of military promotion, an English peerage for himself and a Scottish peerage for his brother before he would come down on the side of Incorporating Union. Similarly the Treasurer-Depute, the earl of Glasgow, appears to have had £20,000 to dispose of from English funds for crossing the palms of the queen's friends in Scotland: if some of it went to paying arrears of salaries it was made fairly plain the recipients would go hungry unless they toed the line.

Had threats and bribery alone been sufficient, however, it would hardly have been necessary for the English to enter into such detailed negotiations as they did, still less for England to make a series of concessions which made the Union eventually much less of an incorporating job than it is usually assumed to be. The course of events in Scotland from 1704 until May 1707 was as follows. Tweeddale succeeded Queensberry in May 1704 when the latter at last proved unable to hold his motley majority together: but Tweeddale, who emerged with some thirty supporters from the Country Party to form the New Party or *Squadron Volante,* was dedicated to a reform of the existing union in the direction of federalism rather than incorporation, and was really crushed by the Alien Act as he could not follow the wish of the queen to press for incorporation. He also proved too weak even to save from summary execution the crew of an English East Indiaman, the *Worcester,* under Captain Green, who were arrested in Scotland on a fabricated charge of piracy against one of the Company of

Scotland's ships. The execution of these miserable scapegoats at the instance of a Scottish lynch mob on the sands of Leith in April 1705 marked the peak of anti-English feeling in the wake of the Alien Act, whose threats had not impressed the population at large whatever they might have done to politicians thinking quietly at home. Tweeddale fell and was replaced by Argyll, who led the government until June and then handed office again to Queensberry. The complex manoeuvrings of the next few months left few parliamentary reputations for honesty and consistency intact: the duke of Hamilton, leader of the Country Party but a man with extensive estates in England, shocked his followers by proposing on 1 September that nominations for appointing commissioners for union should be left to the queen. This had the effect of allowing the government to set up a body in which all favoured incorporation except one, the Jacobite Lockart of Carnwarth. They began to deliberate with their English counterparts in April 1706: on the 4 November, the first article of Union was put to the Scottish parliament and accepted by 115 votes to 83; the whole Treaty was ratified on 16 January 1707 by 110 votes to 67: it came into force on 1 May 1707 and the parliamentary independence of Scotland came to an end.

The terms of the Union, however, show how far it was necessary for England to make concessions to the Scots which in the long run proved a bone in the throat of real incorporation. There was to be free trade and the open admission of the Scots to the English market and to English colonial privileges, which, it was argued by both English and Scottish propagandists, was a great advantage but not really accepted as enough by the Royal Burghs who represented the major part of the formal 'trading interest' and most consistently of all opposed union: but they were bought off by a promise of an Equivalent Fund to boost Scottish development and an undertaking that their particular privileges would stay intact even after the treaty. The church was exempted by special legislation from any threat of amalgamation with the Church of England. The existing law of Scotland was similarly defended, which kept the professions of the lawyers intact. As for the landed classes, the continuation of particular economic privileges granted before the Union was one sop, the granting of 45 seats in the English Commons and 16 seats in the English Lords was another. They also had every expectation that the Scottish privy council would be kept in being after the Union as a theatre for their talents and ambitions, but it was in fact abolished within a year.

The Scottish establishment, therefore, by no means came badly out of the Union. In voting for it they were aware that all bourgeois career patterns were effectively protected from English encroachment, that the gentry and nobility had a political sphere reserved for them, and that economic arguments (which were often stressed in the course of the final debates) favoured entry. They must also have been aware that the alternatives included the danger of English attack and conquest if independence was declared, of civil war between Jacobites and others in the case of a disputed succession, and of the very illusory, shadowy nature of the parliamentary liberty they were called upon to surrender. Even the New Party came round in the course of 1705 and 1706 to supporting Incorporating Union: maybe it was, as one historian has said, 'duped by a promise of handling that part of the Equivalent which related to the losses of the Company of Scotland and also undue representation in the sixteen peers', but one of its members explained in a private letter why men of his sympathies would in the end vote for parliamentary Union – 'Trade with most, Hanover with some, ease and security with others, together with a general aversion to civil discords, intolerable poverty and ... constant oppressions'. It seems a catalogue of good reasons and from their point of view, a fair summary of the national interest.

Who was not asked? The common people of Scotland were neither represented in the Scottish parliament nor listened to by it, though anti-Union petitions and the mobbing and rioting against the pro-union members which went on before the final voting greatly alarmed the government and encouraged its opponents. Sir John Clerk of Penicuik was to write later that 'the articles were confirmed in the Parliament of Scotland contrary to the inclinations of at least three-fourths of the Kingdom': the Jacobites set about making immediate preparations for a rising. When the Union was passed, however, people took it with the greatest calmness: a Jacobite plot of 1708 never got off the ground; the rebellion of 1715 had no popular support in the Lowlands, and very little else suggested passions on the subject.

In the end one is forced to the conclusion that the Union of

Parliaments did not at the time seem of overriding importance to very many Scots. Real independence in the sense of control over foreign policy had gone in 1603. For many years the gentlemen in Parliament House in Edinburgh had seemed to be little better than puppets dancing to the tune of the London government, and nothing since 1703 had encouraged people to regard them very differently. The church mattered more than parliament to most people, and that was to go on: so were the law, the colleges, the schools, the town councils: economic control of most things still rested in the north. Men had estates to manage, farms to farm, goods to sell and ships to sail: London was a long way off and the role of government interference in everyday life was extremely small by modern standards. Most Scots would, quite rightly, have laughed at the idea that the Scottish nation came to an end in 1707. There was more to life and nationality than an assembly of members of parliament, and it was another century at least, perhaps two, before the erosion of what was distinctively Scottish about the Scots reached such a level as to justify serious doubts about national survival: it was the end of an auld sang, perhaps, but it was not yet the end of an auld people.

Books for further reading

General

DICKINSON, W. CROFT *New history of Scotland vol. 1. Scotland from earliest times to 1603* Nelson, 1961.

GRANT, I. F. *The social and economic development of Scotland before 1603* Oliver & Boyd, 1930. o.p.

MACKENZIE, W. C. *The Highlands and Isles of Scotland* Moray Press, 1937. o.p.

MITCHISON, R. *A history of Scotland* Methuen, cased and paperback 1970.

Oxford book of Scottish verse chosen by J. McQueen and T. Scott. O.U.P., 1966.

RAIT, R. S. *The Parliaments of Scotland* Glasgow: Maclehose and Johnstone, 1924. o.p.

SMOUT, T. C. *A history of the Scottish people 1560–1830* Collins, 1969, cased 1969, paperback 1972.

WITTIG, K. *The Scottish tradition in literature* Oliver & Boyd, 1958. o.p.

The Medieval Period   Chapters 1, 2, 3 and 4

BALFOUR-MELVILLE, E. W. M. *James I, King of Scots* Methuen, 1936. o.p.

BARBOUR, J. *The Bruce* trans. and ed. by A. A. H. Douglas. Maclellan, 1964.

BARRON, E. M. *The Scottish war of independence* J. Nisbit, 1934, o.p.

BARROW, G. W. S. *Robert Bruce and the community of the realm of Scotland* Eyre and Spottiswoode, 1965. o.p.

DOUGLAS, G. *Selections* ed. by D. F. C. Coldwell. O.U.P., 1964.

DUNBAR, W. *Poems* ed. by W. M. Mackenzie. Edinburgh: Porpoise Press, 1950. o.p. : Faber, n.e. paperback 1970.

DUNLOP, A. I. *The life and times of James Kennedy, Bishop of St. Andrews* Oliver and Boyd, 1950, o.p.

DUNLOP, A. I. *Scots abroad in the fifteenth century* Historical Association Pamphlet No. 124. 1942.

FERGUSSON, J. *William Wallace, Guardian of Scotland* Stirling: Eneas Mackay, 1938. o.p.

GILLIES, W. *An introduction to Scottish Gaelic literature* Edinburgh: Southside (to be published in 1973).

MACKENZIE, W. M. *The Scottish burghs* Oliver & Boyd, 1949. o.p.

MACKENZIE, W. M. *The medieval castle in Scotland* Methuen, 1927. o.p.

MACKIE, R. L. *King James IV of Scotland* Oliver & Boyd, 1958.

MACQUEEN, J. *Robert Henryson: a study of the major narrative poems* O.U.P., 1967.

NICHOLSON, R. *The Edinburgh history of Scotland Vol. 2 Scotland: the later Middle Ages* Oliver & Boyd (to be published in 1973).

SCOTT, T. *Dunbar* Oliver & Boyd, 1966.

The Sixteenth Century   Chapters 5, 6 and 7

BINGHAM, C. *James V, King of Scots* Collins, 1971.

BROWN, P. HUME *John Knox: a biography* 2 vols. A. & C. Black, 1895. o.p.

COWAN, I. B. *The enigma of Mary Stewart* Gollancz, 1971.

DONALDSON, G. *The Edinburgh history of Scotland. Vol. 3: Scotland: James V to James VII* Oliver & Boyd, 1965.

DONALDSON, G. *The first trial of Mary Queen of Scots* Batsford, 1969.

FRASER, A. *Mary Queen of Scots* Weidenfeld & Nicolson, 1969; Panther Books, 1970.

KNOX, J. *History of the Reformation in Scotland* 2 vols. ed. by W. C. Dickinson. Nelson, 1949.

LEE, M. *John Maitland of Thirlestane* Princeton U.P., 1959.

LYTHE, S. G. E. *The economy of Scotland in its European setting 1550–1625* Oliver & Boyd, 1960.

MATHIESON, W. L. *Politics and religion: study in Scottish history from reformation to revolution* 2 vols. Glasgow: Maclehose & Johnstone, 1902. o.p.

MCEWEN, J. S. *The faith of John Knox* Lutterworth Press, 1961.

RIDLEY, J. G. *John Knox* O.U.P., 1968.

WILLSON, D. H. *James VI and I* (Bedford History) Cape, 1956.

The Seventeenth Century   Chapters 8, 9 and 10

BUCHAN, J. *Montrose* Nelson, 1928. o.p.; Hodder, 1949.

CAMPBELL, W. *The triumph of Presbyterianism* Edinburgh : St Andrews P. 1958. o.p.

DICKINSON, W. C. and others *A source book of Scottish history Vol. III: 1567–1707* Nelson, 1961. o.p.

DONALDSON, G. *Edinburgh history of Scotland Vol. 3: Scotland: James V to James VII* Oliver & Boyd, 1965.

FERGUSON, W. *Edinburgh history of Scotland Vol. 4: Scotland: 1689 to the present* Oliver & Boyd, 1968.

FOSTER, W. R. *Bishop and Presbytery* S.P.C.K., 1958. o.p.

HENDERSON, G. D. *Religious life in seventeenth century Scotland* C.U.P., 1937. o.p.

HOLMES, G. *Britain after the glorious Revolution 1689–1714* Macmillan, cased and paperback 1969.

MACKINNON, J. *The Union of England and Scotland: a study of international history* Longmans, 1896. o.p.

MATHIESON, W. L. *Politics and religion: study in Scottish history from reformation to revolution* 2 vols. Glasgow : Maclehose & Johnstone., 1902. o.p.

PRYDE, G. S. *The Treaty of Union of Scotland and England 1707* ed. Nelson, 1950.

SMOUT, T. C. *Scottish trade on the eve of the Union* Oliver & Boyd 1963.

WEDGWOOD, C. V. *The great rebellion vol. 1. The King's peace* Collins, 1955.

WEDGWOOD, C. V. *The great rebellion vol. 2. The King's war 1641–47* Collins, 1958.

WILLCOCK, J. *The Great Marquess: life and times of Archibald, 8th Earl and 1st (and only) Marquess of Argyll, 1607–1661* Oliphant, 1902. o.p.

Index